Also by Jan Henson Dow

Nonfiction
Writing the Award-Winning Play (with
    Shannon Michal Dow)

Poetry
At the Han-ku Pass

Full-Length Plays
Dark Passages (with Shannon Michal Dow and
    Robert Schroeder, published by Popular Play
    Service)
Dreamers, Shadows, Dreams (with Robert
    Schroeder, published by Popular Play Service)
The Golden Dawn (with Robert Schroeder,
    published by Popular Play Service)
Killing Dante (with Shannon Michal Dow,
    published by Samuel French, Inc.)
The Magistry (with Robert Schroeder, published
    by Popular Play Service)
That Madcap Moon (with Robert Schroeder,
    published by Popular Play Service)

PLAYS THAT POP!
ONE-ACT, TEN-MINUTE, AND MONOLOGUES

PLAYS THAT POP!
ONE-ACT, TEN-MINUTE, AND MONOLOGUES

JAN HENSON DOW
WITH
SHANNON MICHAL DOW, ROBERT SCHROEDER,
AND JIM PEGOLOTTI

Phosphene Publishing Company
Houston, Texas

Plays That Pop!: One-Act, Ten-Minute, and Monologues
© 2016 by Jan Henson Dow
ISBN 10: 0-9851477-6-8
ISBN 13: 978-0-9851477-6-1

The plays in this volume are works of fiction. Names, characters, places, and incidents either are products of the author's imagination or are used as fiction.

Published by
Phosphene Publishing Company
Houston, Texas, USA
phosphenepublishing.com

For
Chris Dow and Shannon Dow
and
Phil Tannenholz

CONTENTS

PRODUCTION OF THE PLAYS IN THIS VOLUME

Due authorship credit must be given on all programs, printing, and advertising for the play.

No one shall commit or authorize any act or omission by which the copyright, or the right to copyright, of these plays may be impaired.

No one may make any changes to these plays in the process of production, or otherwise.

Correspondence and inquiries may be made through the Phosphene Publishing Company website at phosphenepublishing.com.

PLAYS THAT POP!
ONE-ACT, TEN-MINUTE, AND MONOLOGUES

ONE-ACT PLAYS

THE SPIRAL STAIR

A One-Act Drama

by

Jan Henson Dow

PRODUCTION NOTES

CAST OF CHARACTERS

William Butler Yeats — 51, dressed in dark clothing.

Maud Gonne — 50, wearing a long black skirt and a shawl over her head. She is carrying a walking stick and a pouch for holding her things.

TIME
After dark in early November 1918, just before the Armistice (which took place on November 11, 1918). It would be seven years later, in 1925, that Yeats would receive the Nobel Prize for Literature.

SETTING
The entry hall of the Tower at Thoor Ballylee, Ireland, where Yeats and his wife, Georgie Hyde-Lees, are staying. Two arm chairs and a table are Up Center. A blanket or shawl is draped over the chair at Right. The main door from the outside is Off Stage Right. A door to the kitchen is Off Stage Left. The lower part of a spiral stair is Up Left.

For my granddaughters: Sydney Dow, Mariko Dow, and Heather Hauser.

THE SPIRAL STAIR

(SOUND OF THUNDER in the distance. The room is in darkness. A HEAVY KNOCK is heard on the iron knocker at the main door Off Right. The KNOCK is repeated, more insistently. A LIGHT appears on the stair. WILLIAM BUTLER YEATS enters Up Left carrying a lantern. YEATS crosses to the door, hesitates, and then opens it.)

(MAUD GONNE, bent over as if with age, is standing at the door. SHE is wearing a long, black skirt and a dark shawl over her head. The shawl conceals her face. SHE is carrying a walking stick and a pouch for holding HER things.)

MAUD
By the saints, will you let me in then? I am chilled to the bone.

(YEATS steps back and SHE enters. HE closes the door. SHE is obviously cold and tired)

YEATS
What do you want here, old woman?

MAUD
Shelter from the storm.

YEATS
'Tis the dead of night and a lonely road to be out on such a night.

MAUD
Yes, the dead of night and a lonely road surely.
> (SHE staggers as if SHE would fall. YEATS quickly helps
> HER to the large arm chair Up Center Right, against the
> wall. HE takes HER stick and pouch. SHE sits.)

YEATS
Here, rest a while.

> (MAUD sits down and bows HER head in one hand
> as if exhausted. YEATS places the lantern on the table
> by the chair. The lantern sends a feeble glow into the
> shadows of the room.)

YEATS
What are you doing out in the wind and cold, an old woman, and no
one with you? Where were you going, then?

MAUD
Yes, where was I going?
> (As if forgetful.)
Where I must.
> (SHE coughs a wracking cough and coughs again.)
Can you spare a cup of tea for an old woman to warm her bones?

YEATS
Wait here.
> (HE takes the blanket from the chair Up Left. HE
> places the blanket over HER knees.)
Here, this will help to warm you.
> (HE exits Left and returns shortly.)
It won't take long for the water to be boiling. Answer me straight now.
What are you doing out on the roads on such a night and no one with
you? Why have you come here?

MAUD

I told you. I am seeking shelter from the storm.

YEATS

No more riddles. What are you hiding? Who are you?

MAUD

Yes, you may well ask. Who am I?
(SHE coughs.)
Could I have that cup of tea, then, to ease my cough?
(YEATS exits and returns with the cup of tea. HE hands
it to HER, and SHE takes a sip from the cup.)
Ah, that is better. It warms my heart — as you once did, many years
ago.

YEATS

As I once did?

MAUD

(Looking at HIM intently, HER face still in shadows.)
You don't know me then?
(SHE throws back the shawl so that HE can see HER
face.)

YEATS

My God! Maud!
(HE staggers back as if from a blow.)
Is it yourself?

MAUD

The very one you loved so long ago.

YEATS

(HE closes the door to the stair and turns back to
MAUD.)
We must not wake my wife. Georgie is eight months gone with child.
She needs to find her rest.

MAUD

Yes, we all need to find our rest.

YEATS

I never thought to see you here and in the dead of night. What has happened to you?

MAUD

What has happened? Everything! Death and war and loss and the horror of seeing young men die, missing an arm or a leg, their eyes shot out from the living light.

YEATS

I didn't realize. The last letters I had from you were from Paris.

MAUD

From Paris? That was after Spain, I think. It all seems to flow together now. When the German armies rolled westward, the wounded and dying filled the hospitals to overflowing. What the Germans did not kill and maim, the Spanish flu struck down by the thousands. It was too awful to stand by and watch the suffering.

YEATS

God forgive us! At what man's door will we lay the crime of this terrible war?

MAUD

I used to see beauty in war, but death and devastation and destruction have broken my heart. When I became ill, they sent me to the coast. I lay sleepless, night after night, feeling the house shake, hearing the pounding of the big naval guns in the channel. I had to return to Ireland if I was to live. Did you know that I was arrested?

YEATS

I heard you had returned and been arrested and deported to England.

MAUD

They arrested seventy-three of us, men and women. We were held for
months in Holloway Prison, every night in total darkness. It was May,
I think, we were arrested. I forget now.

MAUD

(SHE begins to cough, and then coughs harder, HE
gives HER the cup of tea and SHE drinks, which helps
to stop the coughing. SHE puts the cup on the table.)
All that time, those long, cold nights in prison, and never a letter or a
word from you.

YEATS

When I learned you were arrested, I tried to get word to you, to be
allowed to see you, but they wouldn't let anyone in. The last letters I
had, you were at a hospital in Paris, nursing the wounded from eight in
the morning until eight at night.

MAUD

They were only boys. We patched them up so that they might be sent
back to the slaughter. In my heart has been growing a wild hatred of
this war and all its horrors.

YEATS

They are saying the Armistice will be signed soon.

MAUD

(Very agitated, SHE stands and paces.)
Soon! Soon! It is already too late! My God, a whole generation has been
wiped out!

YEATS

Did you know — Lady Gregory's son was killed in action?

MAUD

Oh, no! That bright boy killed! When?

YEATS

In January. His plane was shot down over the Channel.

MAUD

Her only son! I remember the little boy at Coole Park, running and laughing, his two arms held out, chasing the wild swans.

YEATS

Yes — chasing the wild swans as they wheeled in great broken rings, mounting the sky on their clamorous wings. He met his fate somewhere there among the clouds.

MAUD

This terrible war!

YEATS

You once were committed to war and full of rebellion.

MAUD

I was, once, full of many things.

YEATS

You've changed. I see it in your face.

MAUD

I have seen boys with their lungs eaten out with mustard gas. They cough and cough and cough and spit up their bloody lungs.
            (SHE begins to cough again and again and again.)

YEATS
            (HE tries to comfort HER.)
Is it your old — complaint? Has it come back then?

MAUD

Those long nights in the dark and cold have brought it on. Those long, lonely nights.

(A long pause.)
So — I heard you had married at last, after all these years.

YEATS
I found myself at fifty with no wife and no child. What was I to do?

MAUD
I always urged you to marry.

YEATS
How generous of you, since you would not have me! I begged you
again and again to marry me!

MAUD
I was already married.

YEATS
Were you? Do you call that a marriage?

MAUD
The church certainly did.

YEATS
When did you ever care what anyone thought?

MAUD
Except for you.

YEATS
Then did you know — there was a time I wished you were lying cold
and dead!

MAUD
I do not remember you so bitter. You, too, have changed.

YEATS
They call this the "Great War to End All Wars." I wonder, what will all

those many thousands dead have bought us. I see the next war and the next when drunken soldiers leave the mother, murdered at her door, crawling in her own blood. I think our days are dragon-ridden and I am fearful for tomorrow.

MAUD

When I first met you, you were not afraid of anything. I remember when you were young and eager and full of hope. You once thought poetry could change the world.

YEATS

And you thought anarchy could right the wrongs. For all of that, we are impotent and angry and powerless, and nothing has changed, except we are growing older.

MAUD

I still remember the look of you, that first day, at the home of John O'Leary. You were dressed in shabby clothes, a tall, restless boy with deep-set, dark eyes, a lock of dark hair falling over your forehead.

YEATS

And I thought you the most extravagant creature I had ever seen.

MAUD

I was that, surely, extravagant and willful and proud.

YEATS

I never thought to see in a living woman so great a beauty. It belonged to poetry, to some legendary past.
> How many loved your moments of glad grace,
> And loved your beauty with love false or true,
> But one man loved the pilgrim soul in you,
> And loved the sorrows of your changing face.

You know that I loved you with all my heart. I remember when we were walking together on the beach in Normandy. I asked you one last time to marry me. You refused.

MAUD

Yes, it was the year after my husband was executed — for treason against the British crown.

YEATS

And the year you were free to marry.

MAUD

You don't understand! I received an order from the British War Office. "Madame MacBride will not be allowed to return to Ireland." Not allowed to return to Ireland! My husband dead! An Irish hero and bearing an honored name.

YEATS

How patriotic of you, since you did not honor him or ever love him.

MAUD

That is a cruel thing to say!

YEATS

The truth is often cruel.

MAUD

And you still blame me!

YEATS

Why should I blame you? Only that you filled my days with misery.

MAUD

You should be grateful I did not marry you.

YEATS

Grateful?

MAUD

You had what you needed, a marble statue on a pedestal to live out your old, high dream of Ireland.

YEATS

And that is a cruel thing to say. My old, high, dream of Ireland! Where is it now! "Romantic Ireland's dead and gone. It's with O'Leary in the grave."

MAUD

If I had married you, it would have been the death of you as a poet.

YEATS

And yet — for all the dying, when I look death in the face or climb to the heights of sleep, suddenly I meet your face, as you were that day on the cliffs in Ireland. I held you in my arms, afraid that you would fall or fly away.

MAUD

I have never been so happy as we were that day. How many people can say they have had one single, perfect day?

YEATS

Yes, one single, perfect day, when we were young.

MAUD

And now, we have come to this time and this place.

YEATS

Yes, we have come to this place and this crossroads. If the authorities find out you are here, they will come to arrest you and all with you. They would arrest my wife. She could not survive prison, not in her condition.

MAUD

You needn't worry. I will stay only a short while. Surely the Irish will close ranks as they always have and resist. And I will be with them. Is the storm over then?

YEATS

Yes, the storm is over. You have already said it; we are as we are and the past is over and done. Though it breaks my heart in two, I cannot let you stay here.

MAUD

Cannot let me stay here?

YEATS

I must think of my wife and our unborn child now. They are the hope of the future. I will make up a pallet for you in the kitchen and stir up the fire. In the morning we will see what must be done with you.

MAUD

How generous! I was offered better in the depths of Holloway Prison. I was offered honor and respect as the champion of Ireland. If I endured exile in the cold and the dark of that miserable prison, I can endure a harsher exile now. I do not choose to accept your "kind hospitality."

(SHE throws the blanket at HIS feet.)

YEATS

You are, still, a proud and obstinate and foolish woman!

MAUD

Yes, I have been foolish, surely — as have you. But I thank you for the one cup of tea that warmed my heart.
            (SHE puts on HER shawl, picks up HER walking stick
            and pouch.)
It is a long road ahead, and I must be on my way.
            (SHE turns and quickly exits at RIGHT. YEATS rushes
            to the door.)

YEATS

Maud! Maud! Come back! Come back!

SOUND OF THUNDER

THE END

STRINDBERG TONIGHT

A One-Act Comedy

by

Jan Henson Dow
and
Robert Schroeder

PRODUCTION NOTES

CAST OF CHARACTERS
(In order of appearance)

Jean — Male, late 20s or early 30s. The character in August Strindberg's play, *Miss Julie*, and the actor rehearsing the role, as well as the director of the rehearsal.

Julie — Female, late 20s or early 30s. The character in *Miss Julie* and the actress rehearsing the role.

August Strindberg — Male, of indeterminate age. A manifestation of the author, as vital, manic, and vigorous as he ever was in life. (Note: Since August Strindberg's resurrection is intended as a surprise, the program listing might be "A Gentleman Caller" or some such alternative.)

TIME AND PLACE
The present, in a theater or in a rehearsal space.

THE SET
A stage that is bare except for a table with pages strewn across it, some chairs, and a hall-tree bearing a vintage hat and a long wrap-around skirt.

COSTUMING

Jean: Attractive rehearsal clothing, or perhaps a white blouse and dark trousers of contemporary cut.

Julie: Attractive rehearsal clothing, or perhaps a white blouse and dark trousers of contemporary cut.

Strindberg: White shirt, dark trousers, and a jacket, all reflecting Northern European styling of the 1880s.

AUTHORS' NOTES AND ACKNOWLEDGMENT

Strindberg Tonight is to be performed in a larger-than-life presentational manner, wittily, gracefully, archly. It is never to become naturalistic, psychologically true, or "real." Nor is any exaggeration to become camp or leering overplaying.

The discourse between the two contemporary actors and the shade of August Strindberg calls for an authentic display of a century-wide span of acting styles.

Julie, about 30, is always, in enunciation and manner, "The Actress." Always "on," she exudes charm and charisma. In dress, looks, and carriage, she decorates the stage.

Jean, both an actor and a director, is about 30. He is good looking, a bit of a cynic, and more than a bit egotistical.

Strindberg, a manifestation of the famous author, evokes a manic Presence rather than portraying any given age.

For Shannon Michal Dow and Paul Evans, and in memory of a dear friend, John Eichrodt.

STRINDBERG TONIGHT

(As the audience enter the theater, the stage LIGHTING is that of a rehearsal-ready space.)

(JEAN enters and begins to perform actor's warm-up exercises. HE hoots, HE howls, HE growls. HE stretches, HE becomes limp, HE is a cat and then an ape. Vigorously HE shakes HIS fingers, hands, feet, etc. The more ridiculous these motions, gesticulations, and utterances seem to the lay audience, the better.)

(While HE is warming up, JEAN from time to time glances at his wristwatch disgustedly.)

JEAN
(Looking at HIS wristwatch yet again and speaking in a complaining, whining manner.)
Where is she? She knew call was seven o'clock.
(Impatiently and half-heartedly, HE does more warm-ups, then again complains.)
So, where is she? I gave her a chance to play in Strindberg's *Miss Julie* — a classic role any actress would kill to perform — and where is she?
(HE begins another warm-up exercise but stops almost at once.)
Actresses! Why can't we have plays without actresses?
(Now exuding self-pity.)
What do they expect of me? I'm to star in the role of Jean,
(Pronounced *zhan*: the *zh* sound is that of the *s* in

vision, and the *a* sound is that of the *a* in *palm*.)
and I'm to direct the play, and I'm to put up with that show-off who
thinks she's the star!

JULIE
(Entering, speaking sweetly but acidly.)
Darling! Did you call?

JEAN
My precious! How very good of you to honor our rehearsal with your
presence.

JULIE
(Crossing directly to the hall-tree.)
My dearest darling! I'm only a tiny bit late.

JEAN
But my jewel, you are always a tiny bit late.

JULIE
(Donning the long wrap-around skirt and the hat.)
But my pet, you are always much too early!

JEAN
When I am both starring in a directing one of the greatest plays in
the entire Western world, I am indeed early — and prepared! Shall we
begin our rehearsal?

JULIE
Of course, as soon as I locate and then position my center.
            (SHE performs abbreviated vocal and body exercises as
            HE looks on disgustedly. SHE suddenly stops.)

JEAN
Did you find your center?

JULIE

Yes! And positioned it!

JEAN

I'm so glad. Now, may we begin?

JULIE

Of course.

JEAN

Let's take it from Miss Julie's speech, "How can I face my father," et cetera, et cetera.

JULIE

Of course.
(SHE takes another moment, checking on HER center, and then begins to enunciate theatrically.)
How can I face my father after what you and I have been to each other?

JEAN
(Rehearsing dramatically.)
We haven't been anything to each other!

JULIE

I suppose you expect me to stay under this roof as your mistress! Never!

JEAN

May I remind you: I did not ask you to stay under this roof as my mistress.

JULIE

Then you must take me away from here, from the shame, the dishonor of this affair.

JEAN

I do not call having sex for less than three minutes "an affair."

JULIE

You despise me!

JEAN

Nicely put.

JULIE

Is anyone on earth as wretched as I?

JEAN

You are wretched? You have a family, wealth, position, while I, a mere valet, have the mind of an aristocrat and the body of a Greek God! I'm the one who should be wretched!

JULIE

I should have known! Once a servant, always a servant!

JEAN

Once a fallen woman, always a fallen woman.

JULIE

That's right! Hit me, trample on me, call me names! That's all I deserve for allowing myself to be seduced by a valet! I hate you!

JEAN

And I find you unbearable.

JULIE

There's only one thing we can do.

JEAN

And what's that?

JULIE

We must go abroad, marry, and be miserable.

JEAN

We can be miserable at home.

JULIE

Or we could have a glass of wine, throw it over our right shoulders, and then die.

JEAN

Die! I think it would be better to start a hotel.

JULIE

You don't want to die with me?

JEAN

I don't even want to live with you.

JULIE

Don't you know what you owe the woman you've ruined?

JEAN

Marriage and divorce?

JULIE

This is what I get for sacrificing my honor. If only you loved me.

JEAN

Love? I think you must be ill.

JULIE

Help me! Tell me where to go!

JEAN

I would like to tell you where to go, but I suggest you stay here and keep quiet.

JULIE

But you and I are so devastatingly attractive, it might happen again.

JEAN

Yes, I'm afraid so.

JULIE

There might be little "consequences."

JEAN

Little "consequences!" I never thought of that!

JULIE

Men never think of consequences.

JEAN

Then you must go abroad.

JULIE

I must go abroad? What about "we?"

JEAN

No, you must go alone. I know women. Once you've sinned, you feel you might as well go on doing it.

JULIE

I suppose men don't want to go on doing it!

JEAN

Think of the little "consequences!" No, you must go alone.

JULIE

But what shall I tell my father?

JEAN

Write and tell him everything, except that it was me.

JULIE

Should I, also, tell him that you persuaded me to abscond with his funds?

JEAN

My God, no! Just send him a card from the Swiss Alps. "Having a wonderful time. Wish you were here."

JULIE

I'll go, if you come with me.

JEAN

Are you out of your mind? The next day it would be in all the headlines. "Miss Julie elopes with her father's valet!" I'd never live it down.

JULIE

Then I can't go, and I can't stay. This is a pretty pickle!

JEAN

Women who discuss pickles are very vulgar.

JULIE

When the police arrive, they will think you are vulgar.

JEAN

The police?

JULIE

Yes. When my father finds his desk broken open and accuses you, he will call the police.

JEAN

But you took the money.

JULIE

A father can't accuse his own daughter. It isn't done. A valet is a much more suitable choice for a thief.

JEAN

I never thought of that!

JULIE

Much better to make an end to it all and come with me.

JEAN

That would not make an end to it all. No! There's only one thing to do.

JULIE

And what is that?

JEAN

You, a lady, have disgraced yourself! You have stolen from your father and have slept with his valet! You must confess and then commit suicide. It's the only noble thing to do.

JULIE

Why must I be noble? Why don't you confess and commit suicide?

JEAN

A valet needn't be noble. It's the one advantage of being a valet.

JULIE

Oh, I see what you mean. But isn't suicide rather messy?

JEAN

Can't you ever think of anyone else? It's the only way our for both of us.
            (HE hands JULIE an imaginary razor.)
Take this razor and go!

JULIE
            (Takes the imaginary razor but hesitates.)
Tell me again to go.

JEAN

There is no other way to end it! Go out to the barn and. . . .
> (HE makes an elaborate gesture across his throat and a
> sound as if slitting his throat.)

JULIE

You mean. . . ?
> (SHE makes the same gesture and sound.)

JEAN

Exactly! Go!
> (A reluctant JULIE starts to exit, then hesitates.)

Go!
> (JULIE exits)

My God! What if her father should ring the bell? What if the police
should come and accuse me? What if she doesn't commit suicide. . . ?
What will happen to me?
> (The bell RINGS. JEAN jumps.)

It's too late! All is lost!
> (JEAN freezes in despair.)

> (JULIE reenters, pulling off her hat and hurling it
> across the stage. SHE is now her very own self — the
> haughty, narcissistic actress — and is no longer playing
> Miss Julie.)

JULIE

I cannot stand this hat another minute! Or this gown! I keep tripping
over it!
> (SHE removes the gown and is now dressed in HER
> rehearsal clothing.)

JEAN

> (Now the director and actor — no long the character
> in the Strindberg play.)

No! No! No! You do not enter again! Go off stage!

JULIE

Off stage?

JEAN

Yes, my sweet. Off stage! The whole mood is destroyed if you come back on. The audience must believe you are committing suicide.

JULIE

Committing suicide?

JEAN

Yes, my precious. With the razor. You are slitting your wrists with the razor!

JULIE

With a razor? Ugh! How messy! I would never use a razor. I don't like the ending of this play.

JEAN

By, my dear one, it is the way the play ends.

JULIE

But, darling, I don't like it, and I won't play it, and that's that!

JEAN

Now, my jewel, let's not get testy.

JULIE

I'm tired of women being tragic. . . ! You've always given me such freedom to develop my roles — such space to be creative. You always let me do exactly as I please. You are a brilliant director!

JEAN

Well, that's certainly true.

JULIE

You know audiences don't want all that soul searching and committing suicide. It's too much like real life. . . . Just think of it: Under your brilliant direction, this dreary old tragedy could be an absolutely divine romantic romp!

JEAN

A romantic romp! Just the thing!

JULIE

I've always wanted to write a play — especially someone else's. Now let me see — I have it! I could elope with the valet, only to discover — you're really a prince! In disguise!

JEAN

A prince in disguise! I like that!

JULIE

You could be — the Prince of Mauritania. You would wear this marvelous scarlet uniform with shiny medals and padded shoulders.

JEAN

Padded shoulders! I like that!

JULIE

We could sing a duet, under the stars.

JEAN

A duet! Under the stars. . . ! But the only music in Strindberg's play is when the others are folk-dancing — and we're in the bedroom doing a duet, but not to a tune.

JULIE

Maybe we could sing while we. . . .

JEAN

I'd need extra pay.

JULIE

Oh, pooh. . . ! Oh! I have it! I have it! I could wear a black lace gown, cut very low — with a silver sash and a very red rose clutched in my teeth.

JEAN

Your teeth?

JULIE

You discover that I am a gypsy dancing girl in disguise.

JEAN

A gypsy dancing girl! And I'm a prince?

JULIE

No, you are a toreador! El Toro!
                    (SHE dances the dodging of the bull.)
You wear a scarlet cape and very tight tights. Of course, that will be a problem — but you can cover it with the scarlet cape.

JEAN

A scarlet cape!

JULIE

And you can assume marvelous poses! In place, so you won't be moving about, distracting the audience. I shall dance!

JEAN

With all eyes on you.

JULIE

Not when my lover discovers us together. He tries to stab me — so you challenge him to a duel to defend my honor.

JEAN

A duel? I thought this was a romantic romp!

JULIE

It is! You both are killed!

JEAN

I — think I've heard this plot before. It's — one of those Italian things. Outdoors. With music. Certainly not Strindberg!

JULIE

Outdoors? With music? Oh, how inconvenient. . . ! I have it! I have it! What a brilliant idea! Just think of it! This could be a beautiful little murder mystery! Indoors! No music! Bodies falling out of closets and discovered in window seats! It would mean a long run and then a tour!

JEAN

A long run!

JULIE

Maybe even a starring role — in a movie!

JEAN

A starring role! In a movie!

JULIE

You could direct. I would be the star.

JEAN
(Disappointed.)

Oh.

JULIE

I could murder the valet and — no! The cook could murder my father and the valet. There's never been a murder mystery where the cook did it. The butler, yes. But think of it — the cook! She could put something dastardly in their food!

JEAN

Too realistic.

JULIE

Oh, no. I have it! The father could murder the cook and the valet and make it look like the valet did it!

JEAN

But if the valet is murdered, how could he be the murderer?

JULIE

That's what makes it a mystery! Oh, no! I have it! We'll let the audience decide who did it! In fact, we'll improvise the whole play!

JEAN

Improvise the whole play! What a brilliant idea!

(JULIE begins to improvise. SHE looks into an imaginary hope chest. SHE overreacts to what SHE sees and slams the imaginary lid.)

JULIE

Oh, my God!

JEAN

What is it?

JULIE

A body in the hope chest!

JEAN

(Looking in the chest and quickly closing the lid.)
Good Lord! A body in the hope chest! Is it dead?

JULIE

Very!

JEAN

But who killed it?

JULIE

The valet!

JEAN

But I am the valet!

JULIE

In disguise! You are the cook disguised as the valet.

JEAN

I am?

JULIE

But you won't get away with this!
            (SHE points HER finger at HIM as if it is a gun.)
What do you think this is?

JEAN

A finger disguised as a gun?

JULIE

You think you are so clever. Do you really think you are the real cook?

JEAN

. . . disguised as the valet!

JULIE

Exactly. But I am the real cook.

JEAN

But I thought. . . .

JULIE

You thought! You were wrong! You posed as the cook in order to disguise yourself as the valet.

JEAN

Then you are. . . ?

JULIE

Yes, you know who I really am. That can mean only one thing!

JEAN

I am the valet?

JULIE

The valet?
                    (SHE laughs insanely.)
Do you expect me to believe that? The valet is dead!

JEAN

In the hope chest?

JULIE

There is no hope chest. That is a window seat disguised as a hope chest!

JEAN

Then who is this?
                    (HE opens an imaginary closet door.)

JULIE

The body in the closet?

JEAN

Of course.
                    (THEY watch an imaginary body slowly fall to the floor.)

JULIE

It can only be — oh, my God! It is! Then it was you who killed him!

JEAN
(Pointing HIS finger at HER as if it were a pistol.)
And what do you think this is?

JULIE
Do you take me for a fool? That is obviously a finger!

JEAN
Wrong! Take that!
(HE shoots HER with his finger.)
Pow! Pow! Pow!

JULIE
(Standing tall — triumphantly unharmed.)
You forgot one thing! Your finger is filled with fake bullets — while mine is loaded with lethal bullets that leave large holes! Take that!
(SHE shoots HIM with HER finger.)
Pow!
(HE reacts to a hit and begins to circle away from HER.)
And that!
(SHE shoots HIM again with HER finger.)
Pow!
(HE reacts to a hit in HIS side and is now in a downward spiral.)
And that!
(SHE shoots HIM yet again with HER finger.)
Pow! Pow!
(HE reacts to a hit in HIS posterior extremity.)

JEAN
(Sinking to the floor.)
Who — are — you?

JULIE
(As SHE triumphantly puts HER foot on HIS fallen body.)
I am the real valet.

JEAN
(As HE lies dying.)
Then — who — am — I?

JULIE
Miss Julie disguised as the cook posing as the valet.

JEAN
Good Lord!
(HE dies elaborately.)

JULIE
(Blowing the smoke off the tip of her finger.)
I think that played rather well.

JEAN
(Standing)
It was smashing!

STRINDBERG
(From the audience area.)
Smashing?

JULIE
Brilliant!

STRINDBERG
Brilliant?

JULIE
So brilliant that . . .

JEAN
. . . we'll rewrite the whole play!

STRINDBERG
(Advancing toward the stage.)
Rewrite the whole play?

JEAN and JULIE
We'll be stars!

STRINDBERG
Stars?

JULIE
There's a strange echo in here. . . .

STRINDBERG
Rewrite my classic play?! Don't let her get away with that!

JULIE
(Shading HER eyes and looking into the audience
area.)
Who is that?

JEAN
I don't know
(Shouting in the direction of the voice.)
Look here! This is a rehearsal!

STRINDBERG
Do you call this a rehearsal?

JEAN
I just did call it a rehearsal.

STRINDBERG
(Now on stage.)
Hand her the razor and order her to go offstage!

JEAN
(To JULIE.)
Take this razor and go!

JULIE
You both know what you can do with that razor — darlings!
(To STRINDBERG.)
Who are you?

STRINDBERG
Madam, I am August Strindberg! I am the author! Without me, there
would be no play!

JULIE
(Aside to JEAN.)
The author! But I thought the author of *Miss Julie* was dead! No
royalties, you said. No playwright interfering with our creativity!

JEAN
(Aside to JULIE.)
Just like a playwright: dead and doesn't know it!
(To STRINDBERG, straightening him out.)
You are dead, you know — old chap!

STRINDBERG
Of course I'm dead! But when I heard what you were doing with my
gem of a play, I rolled over in my grave, and here I am!

JEAN
Yes. . . . So I see.
(Altogether taken aback — appealing to JULIE for
help.)
It is the author. He's here!

JULIE
Oh, my God! the actual author. . . ? Well, there's only one thing to
do.

(After a pause to adjust, speaking with excessive sweetness.)
I'm so glad you're here! I absolutely adore working with playwrights!

                              JEAN
Developing the play!

                              JULIE
Making darling little changes here and there.

                              JEAN
Rewriting whole scenes — all of us pen in hand!

                              JULIE
Changing the ending. We always change the ending.

                              JEAN
Striking out the stage directions.

                              JULIE
And improvising new lines — especially mine!

                              JEAN
And, of course, changing the setting! Sweden, where you set the play, is imply passé these days. All those dismal Ingmar Bergman movies and all. . . . I've been thinking of setting your *Miss Julie* in Venice, in Othello's time. All that water, water just — everywhere! It's so symbolic. . . .! Or, no! I have it! We'll set the play in Brazil in, say, 1890! Think of the social significance! The valet can be one of the slaves that Brazil had just set free! Midsummer Eve can become Carnival time! We'll call Jean the valet João, and Miss Julie will become Doña Julia!

                              JULIE
What a darling idea!
                    (Attempting HER erratic notion of a Brazilian accent.)
Doña Julia! I will be — marvelous!

JEAN

So you see, old chap — we're at your service!

STRINDBERG

(Aghast, unable to absorb it all.)

Rewriting! Striking out! Improvising! Venice! Brazil. . . ! I would like to remind you that my play needs no changing or improvising! It has been produced for the last one hundred years.

JEAN

Yes, that's about how long it takes to get a play produced — in its fully developed form, that is. One begins with a staged reading or two, all of us making little changes here and there. . . .

JULIE

Lots of workshopping, at Equity scale. . . .

JEAN

The director receiving his share of the royalties for life, of course. . . .

JULIE

As does the star! Theater is a collaborative art, you know. . . .

STRINDBERG

If a playwright were not already dead, the likes of the two of you would surely kill him.

JEAN

(Aside to JULIE.)

We certainly hope so — makes getting to opening night so much easier when the author is finally out of the way!

JULIE

(Aside to JEAN.)

I know what you mean.

(Again, ever so sweetly.)

Are you really August Strindberg, the famous playwright — in the flesh?

STRINDBERG
In the spirit, so to speak.

JULIE
I am so thrilled! I have so wanted to discuss you and your work. What do you think of the way I play it?

STRINDBERG
Madam, I do not wish to think of you at all.

JULIE
Oh? Isn't that a bit churlish? After all, I have the most marvelous idea for altogether rewriting you dear little play.

STRINDBERG
My dear little play! Madam, I am astounded!

JULIE
I knew you'd like the idea! We'll make it a murder mystery, and at each performance, the audience can decide who did it.

STRINDBERG
Madam, I would like to remind you that I am the author, and you are merely an actress. Actresses are never expected to improve the play! One only hopes they don't destroy it!

JULIE
Well, this play needs improving. Audiences find tragedies depressing.

STRINDBERG
What do they expect — cheerful tragedies?

JULIE
What a marvelous idea!

STRINDBERG
You, madam, were hired to rehearse — not to spew out nonsense!

JULIE

I'm tired of rehearsing! I want to star!

STRINDBERG

Get that strumpet off the stage!

JEAN

I can't. She won't go.

STRINDBERG
(Mocking.)
"I can't. She won't go. . . ." Good God! That's no way to handle women!
Take control! Use a firm hand! Like this!
(To JULIE.)
Go off stage. I tell you! Take this razor and go! At this very moment you
are slashing your wrists in the barn!

JULIE

In the barn? How absurd!

STRINDBERG

Absurd? What do you mean, absurd? I tell you, you are slashing your
wrists in the barn!

JULIE

I would never slash my wrists. But if I did, it would certainly not be
in a barn. I might put on my favorite negligee and take just a few pills.
Not too many, mind you. Just enough to create a scene. But suicide in
a barn? Never!

STRINDBERG

What do you mean, "never?" I am the author. If I tell you to slash your
wrists, you will do as I say!

JULIE

I have no intention of doing as you say any longer. I am an actress with
a mind of my own!

STRINDBERG
(Mocking JULIE.)
"I am an actress with a mind of my own!" You have no mind of your own — no thoughts of your own — no words of your own! Every thought, every word, every deed are what I have put into your silly head!

JULIE
And if I have silly head, who put it there? You! Well, I don't choose to be silly any longer. I am a new woman with new thoughts and ideas.

JEAN
(To STRINDBERG.)
See? What did I tell you?

JULIE
You came back to life in the wrong century! I have sex once, mind you, with this — nincompoop — and I am expected to kill myself? Come to think of it, it wasn't much to live for. No rockets went off, or anything like that.

JEAN
I resent that! If was you who pursued me!

JULIE
I pursued you? Read the script! The valet has been spying on Miss Julie ever since I was an innocent child of ten and you were a snotty brat!

JEAN
Well, you are no longer an innocent child of ten. If you ask me, you are a neurotic bitch.

JULIE
I — a neurotic bitch? How dare you?

JEAN
I saw you with my own eyes, when you thought I wasn't looking,

making your fiancé jump over your riding crop and then hitting him with it. For shame!

STRINDBERG

For shame!

JEAN

He was positively foaming at the mouth!

STRINDBERG

She obviously has a weak and degenerative brain.

JEAN

You made him lick your boots!

JULIE

Lick my boots?
                    (Aside to JEAN.)
That does sound kinky. Did I really do that?

JEAN
                    (Aside to JULIE.)
As much as. Read the script.

JULIE

Well, he didn't have to do it. I didn't hold a gun to his head.

JEAN

Nevertheless, it was in very poor taste.

JULIE

Of course, being born in a hovel makes you an arbiter of good taste.

JEAN

I have a proper respect for my position, which is more than I can say for some people I know.

STRINDBERG
(In a congratulatory tone.)
You may be only a valet, but you have the instincts of an aristocrat.

JEAN
Thank you. My thoughts exactly.

JULIE
The instincts of an aristocrat? You are both snobs! Respect for my position! What a laugh! In your world, a woman could choose to be a wife — or a servant — or a streetwalker. . . ! What kind of choice is that?

JEAN
The only proper choice.

STRINDBERG
Respectable women should only be seen in the bedroom, the kitchen, or the streets.

JULIE
In that order?

JEAN
See? All women ever think of is love and sex, sex and love! That's the trouble with women! I have a higher ambition.

JULIE
Yes, and what is that, pray tell?

JEAN
To become a headwaiter.

JULIE
A headwaiter? You call that a higher position?

JEAN

And what is wrong with being a headwaiter? We actors need a legitimate profession.

JULIE

I am tired of waiters, and I am tired of waiting! If we women are to make sense of the world, we must start now! And that means not waiting for men who think the solution to the world's problems is suicide — or becoming a headwaiter! You men have been in power long enough!

JEAN and STRINDBERG

Power?!

STRINDBERG

We have never been in power! We have always been controlled by castrating women! First our mothers tell us not to play with our wee wees — then, when we no longer can play with our wee wees, our mistresses turn to someone else! I wish you would leave my wee wee alone!

JULIE

I never touched your wee wee! That's all you men thing about — getting it up and sticking it somewhere! Look at what you have done to the world! You're dinosaurs! Dodo birds! You're already extinct, and you just don't know it. It's time for new thoughts, new women, and new men. Both of you had better wake up or I'll just leave you behind!

JEAN

You leave me? After what we've been to each other?

STRINDBERG

You never were anything to her. I saw her first!

JEAN

Yes, but I had her first!

STRINDBERG
What do you mean, "had?"

JEAN
Had! In the biblical sense! Is that plain enough? What do think we were doing in my bedroom? Folk dancing?

STRINDBERG
You never had her! I never intended that you actually have her!

JULIE
Saving her for yourself?

STRINDBERG
(Ignoring JULIE, concentrating on JEAN.)
You have no proof that you had her!

JEAN
I came out of the bedroom smoking a cigarette and smiling. What more proof would you need?

STRINDBERG
You can't find good servants anymore!

JEAN
You know-it-all authors think we actors are nothing but servants! "Stand here! Move there! Speak up! Sit down!" You can't keep us actors enslaved forever! Actors of the world, stand up for your rights! You have nothing to lose but your Equity card!

JULIE
Bravo! That's really rather a brilliant speech, coming from you. Did you make that up?

JEAN
Yes. I frequently make up my own speeches. Keeps the other actors on their toes. Sometimes I surprise myself with my brilliant, spontaneous utterances.

STRINDBERG

Brilliant utterances, indeed! A playwright spends a year perfecting a line, which an actor erases with the snap of a finger!

JEAN

You're mixing your metaphors, old man. Which an actor wipes away with a slip of his tongue!

JULIE

You're just jealous — because the actors always have the last word!

STRINDBERG

I am never jealous!

JULIE

You are! I think that's very funny!

STRINDBERG

For your information, I do not write comedy!

JULIE

But the world needs laughter.

STRINDBERG

Life is a tragedy! I have suffered! You have suffered! And by Lucifer, the audience is going to suffer, too!

JULIE

I'm sure you've suffered, Mr. Strindberg. Did you have four, or was it five, wives?! I'm sure they suffered, too.

STRINDBERG

I did not have five wives! You don't know a thing about my wives!

JEAN

They were all actresses — that's all I need to know.

STRINDBERG

I could write a book about actresses.

JULIE

You did. Full of false accusations and sophomoric self-pity — and not one shred of understanding about women.

STRINDBERG

I can tell you all that needs to be understood about women: They are morally, mentally, and biologically inferior to men.

JULIE

Inferior to men?

STRINDBERG

Women are an odd species — somewhere between a man and a monkey.

JEAN

Something like the missing link?

STRINDBERG

Precisely. And the "new women" is the worst of the lot. Like greedy children, they want it all. They want marriage and a career. Family and freedom. Leave home and like it. Who do they think they are? Men?

JULIE

What the new women needs is the new man.

STRINDBERG

Spare me. If there is anything worse than the new woman, it is the new man . . .
        (Gestures toward JEAN.)

JEAN

Don't look at me!

STRINDBERG

. . . these namby-pamby, limp-wristed nincompoops, who wouldn't
know their wee wees from their wah wahs!

JEAN

I do, too, know my wee wee from my wah wah!

STRINDBERG

When I created the two of you, I must have been out of my mind!

JULIE

You were, frequently.

STRINDBERG

Well, who drove me out of my mind? All those wives! They would drive
any man mad. . . ! All I wanted was an Ideal Relationship — and what
did I get? Marriage!

JEAN

An Ideal Relationship! What would that be like?

STRINDBERG

Very simple. Men and women should never dine together, never live
together, and never be seen together in public.

JEAN

Much like a modern marriage.

STRINDBERG

All I ever wanted — ever needed — was the Ideal Woman. Why is that
too much to ask? But where is she to be found?

JEAN

Have you tried the "Personals" in the *Village Voice*?

JULIE

I shall play the part of your Ideal Woman — to teach you a lesson.

JEAN
You! The Ideal Woman?

STRINDBERG
You?! Absurd!

JULIE
The least a playwright can do is give an actress an audition.

STRINDBERG
Oh, all right. . . ! My Ideal Woman would have to have long blonde curls.

JULIE
(Producing a blonde wig as if by magic.)
I always keep a spare, just in case.

STRINDBERG
And you will have to have. . . .
(HE pauses, embarrassed.)

JULIE
Yes. . . ?

STRINDBERG
An admiring little voice.

JULIE
(Both amused and incredulous.)
An admiring little voice?

STRINDBERG
That's not it! Do you want to be my Ideal Woman, or not?

JULIE
Sorry, I'll have another go at it.
(Speaking now in an admiring little voice.)
Oh, you must be the great author!

STRINDBERG
Yes, that's very nicely done, but. . . .

JULIE
But. . . ?

STRINDBERG
You must have wide, very blue, rather silly eyes.

JULIE
Like this?
      (SHE stares at HIM brightly, with wide, rather silly eyes.)

STRINDBERG
That's — very nicely done, too, but. . . .

JULIE
But. . . ?

STRINDBERG
My Ideal Woman would have to have. . . .
      (Hesitating, embarrassed.)

JULIE
Yes. . . ?

STRINDBERG
Would have to have big . . .
      (HE cups his two hands and holds them under his chest.)
. . . but you can never manage that!

JULIE
      (With hasty downward glance.)
There are some things we'll just have to improvise.
      (JULIE retrieves the long skirt, dons it, and pulls on the

wig. SHE then stands, visibly changing HER center —
getting into character.)

JEAN

She's always been a quick study.

STRINDBERG

I could have guessed that.
              (JULIE strikes a pose — now the Ideal Woman.)
Hm-m-m . . . and what is your name, my dear?

JULIE

              (Vacuously.)
My name? What is my name?

STRINDBERG

Charming! She doesn't even know her own name! I shall call you —
Galatea!

JEAN

How original!

JULIE

Galatea! Oh! My name is Galatea!
              (HER eyes seeming now to be very wide, very blue,
              and rather silly.)
Oh, I've so wanted to meet a real genius.

STRINDBERG

Just think of me as God.

JULIE

Oh, I will. . . ! My — God!

JEAN

I'm going to be ill.

JULIE

Oh, and you must be his. . . .

JEAN

Just think of me as — his Son!

JULIE

Oh, how very talented of you!

JEAN

She is rather charming.

STRINDBERG

Intelligent as well as charming.

JULIE
(To STRINDBERG.)
I hope you won't think me too forward if — if I. . . .

STRINDBERG

Yes, my dear child, do go on.

JULIE

Dare I tell you?

STRINDBERG

Dare.

JULIE

That I admire you?

STRINDBERG

You may.

JULIE

And I admire your — Son.

JEAN
She is quite charming, actually.

JULIE
May I cast off all reserve?

STRINDBERG
Cast off!

JULIE
And tell you with trembling lips and a flashing glance that I must love you or die.

JEAN
Love — him?

JULIE
I must fall on my knees and kiss your genius hands a thousand, million times!
>   (SHE falls at STRINDBERG'S feet and begins ravenously to kiss HIS hands.)

STRINDBERG
And I must look into your wise, true eyes and press my lips to your wise, clear brow — the purest kiss I have ever known!
>   (STRINDBERG stoops and deigns to pull HER forehead to HIS lips — kissing her brow.)

JEAN
Kissing — him?

STRINDBERG
>   (As HE gently draws JULIE to HER feet.)

Rise up, my young lioness, shake your golden mane, and shoot lightning from your starry eyes. . . ! Tear yourself loose from this loathsome menagerie — out to the fresh, free forest where a heart, a head, and a bosom await you and a love which can never die.

JULIE

Oh! To the forest!

STRINDBERG

Yes! To the forest!

JULIE

To the — forest? Oh!

STRINDBERG

Is there anything wrong, my precious?

JULIE

I was just wondering — a very small wonder. Are there any — theaters
in the forest?

STRINDBERG

Theaters?

JULIE

I have always had one teeny, tiny, secret desire — dare I name it?

JEAN

I have this teeny, tiny feeling of having been here before.

STRINDBERG

What is your teeny, tiny, secret desire, my treasure?

JULIE

To be . . .

JEAN

. . . or not to be . . .

JULIE

. . . and actress!

STRINDBERG

An actress! We have all been here before.

(HE is struggling to rekindle dampened fires.)

But of course. Of course, she shall be an actress. I shall create for her a theater where she shall sit on the throne of my genius.

JEAN

A pointed promise.

STRINDBERG

Together, we shall acquire wings and waft away from this weary world. We shall go forth into the infinite unknown where our souls may passionately and eternally embrace — with no need to be ashamed or to ask leave of anyone else on earth!

JULIE

Except my husband.

STRINDBERG

Your husband!

JEAN

They always have a husband.

JULIE

Yes, my husband. But he has no objections to my being intimate with other men — so long as I remain chaste.

STRINDBERG

Chaste?!

JEAN

Chas –ed. As in pursued?

JULIE

Chaste! As in impenetrable.

STRINDBERG

Chaste? As in impenetrable? Is he insulting my manhood? Who does he think he is?

JULIE

My husband.

STRINDBERG

Then you must leave him at once!

JULIE

But mark the contradictions in all of this, the duality of my feelings. I discover that I love him and I love you. I love you both, and I cannot live another day without either of you. What am I to do?

JEAN

The razor!

STRINDBERG

File for divorce immediately!

JULIE

My husband and I?

STRINDBERG

All three of us. The last I remember, my wife was driving me mad!

JULIE

You never told me you had a wife.

STRINDBERG

It's the plural form — wives.

JULIE

Wives? In the plural?

STRINDBERG
Unluckily, they were in the flesh.

JEAN
Wives! In the plural! And in the flesh. . . ! I understand why thoughts of razors and suicide would take form in your genius head.

STRINDBERG
They drove me to it!

JEAN
Whereas, you did none of the driving.

STRINDBERG
None!

JULIE
(Forgetting to use HER admiring little voice.)
That is very hard to believe!

STRINDBERG
What?!

JULIE
(Quickly recovering.)
Oh, I will be your beloved little princess.

STRINDBERG
Born to sit on the throne of my genius.

JULIE
We shall fulfill my calling.

STRINDBERG
You shall become the greatest actress in the land.

JULIE

And the greatest authoress.

STRINDBERG

Authoress?

JULIE

Those wives who tormented you so — they did not share in your genius, composing, creating, writing with you as your beloved companion and collaborator!

STRINDBERG

Collaborator?

JULIE

At your side, I shall become the greatest actress, authoress, and geniusess!

STRINDBERG

Authoress. . . ?! Geniusess. . .?! But my treasure. . . .

JEAN

You mean "treasuress."

STRINDBERG

My little princess! You mustn't trouble your little head about — being an authoress!

JULIE
                    (HER voice no longer little, or admiring.)
Trouble my little head?

STRINDBERG

Yes! Ideal Women are only meant to have admiring little thoughts in their admiring little heads.

JULIE
(Interrupting as SHE removes HER skirt and HER
wig.)
I don't think I was meant to be an Ideal Woman. All this bliss is more
than I can bear. I need strife to find happiness.

STRINDBERG
You're about to change, aren't you? I can see it!
(To JEAN.)
They always change! We're not even married, and already we're
miserable!

JULIE
Oh! I have it! What a brilliant idea! We'll be miserable together — and
together write a play about our misery!

JEAN
A miserable play!

STRINDBERG
Write a play together? Nothing is ever enough! They not only want in
your pants — and in your pockets — they want in your head! In your
soul! They want to pick away at your genius. . . ! There's no such thing
as the Ideal Woman. She is a hoax!

JEAN
A sham!

STRINDBERG
A charlatan!

JEAN
A charade!

STRINDBERG
A hussy!

JEAN

A Jezebel!

STRINDBERG

A Hedda Gabler!

JEAN

A Lady Macbeth!

JULIE

Yes, those are always the best parts. Now — don't get so upset. You must both learn to relax.

STRINDBERG
(Very tense.)
We are relaxed!

JEAN
(Very tense.)
Look how relaxed! What do you call this?

JULIE

Definitely Type A. Now breathe deeply. . . .

JEAN

How can we breathe deeply . . .

STRINDBERG

. . . when we are gritting our teeth?

JULIE

That's just it. You're all tense. You must learn to relax.
            (SHE demonstrates.)
Hang loose!
            (JULIE crosses to JEAN and places HER hands on
            HIS shoulders.)
Let yourself go!

(SHE massages and moves HIS shoulders in a rhythmic motion.)

Like this!

(HER hands continue a rhythmic stroking.)

There! Doesn't that feel better?

JEAN

Much better! You are a geniusess!

(HE stands wiggling and undulating, enjoying HIS relaxed state.)

JULIE

(Crossing to STRINDBERG.)

Now! Your turn!

STRINDBERG

Remember, I've been dead since 1912. If you bend me, I might break.

JULIE

Look at it this way: What have you got to lose?

(JULIE places HER hands on STRINDBERG'S shoulders.)

Let yourself go!

(SHE massages and moves HIS shoulders in a rhythmic motion.)

Like this!

(HER hands move down to HIS biceps as she continues the rhythmic stroking.)

Feel those biceps! You're so strong — for a writer!

(As JULIE continues to stroke STRINDBERG'S biceps and shoulders and then moves down over HIS body, BOTH experience a sexual energy igniting, then building.)

Feel that strong, firm body! You're so firm — for a writer!

JEAN

He'd like you to think so.

(JULIE draws STRINDBERG into a frontal embrace. BOTH react to an irrepressible, galvanic sexual arousal.)

JULIE

Oh! He is!

(SHE suddenly pushes HERSELF away from HIM.)

What is your astrological sign?

JEAN

I knew it! I knew it! If you answer her, it's all over.

STRINDBERG

Aquarius. Why do you ask?

JULIE

If we are to live together, we must be compatible.

STRINDBERG

Live together? Compatible?

JEAN

She tried that on me! Don't let her get away with it!

JULIE

I'm an Aries! Aries and Aquarius! We'll get along marvelously — from time to time.

STRINDBERG

Why would I want to live with you? You think you are as smart as men.

JULIE

True.

STRINDBERG

You think you can be as independent as men.

JULIE

True.

STRINDBERG

Women like you don't want marriage — you want a merger!

JEAN

I'd say more of a hostile takeover.

JULIE

Someone who was as miserable in marriage as you were should be ready to try something else.

JEAN

The razor?

STRINDBERG

I rather like my old habits.

JULIE

I know, but they just don't play anymore. They will have to go. I have changed, and you will have to change, too, my dear.

STRINDBERG

You called me "my dear."

JULIE

Yes.

STRINDBERG

Well — exactly what do you propose?

JULIE

There's something both men and women want that never goes out of style.

STRINDBERG

And what is that?

JULIE

Love and trust and caring.

STRINDBERG

Love?

JULIE

Yes.

STRINDBERG

Trust?

JULIE

Yes.

STRINDBERG

Caring?

JULIE

Yes, but. . . .

JEAN

There's always a "but."

JULIE

There must be no more ordering me about.

STRINDBERG

When did I ever order you about?

JULIE

No scenes in the kitchen. No suicide.

STRINDBERG

I defy you to write a play without a kitchen or a suicide!

JULIE

Now you're getting tense again!

STRINDBERG

(In a softer tone.)
I defy you to write a play without. . . .

JULIE

Love and trust and caring?

STRINDBERG

Yes, love, if one can find it. And trust, if one can find it. And caring, if one can find it.

JULIE

In one's own heart — for starters?

STRINDBERG

Yes, in one's own heart . . . if one has the courage.

JULIE

Courage?

STRINDBERG

Yes, courage! The courage to seek out human truth — one's own truth — without fear as to where that search might lead. That takes courage.

JULIE

Courage.

STRINDBERG

The courage to go all the way to the edge of the world and not worry about whether we ever get back again!

JULIE

The courage to go all the way to the edge of the world and not worry about whether we ever get back again. You said "we."

STRINDBERG

Yes.

JULIE

Might we fall off the edge of the world?

STRINDBERG

Yes.

JULIE

Might there be dragons?

STRINDBERG

There will surely be dragons. Are you ready?

JULIE

Yes.

STRINDBERG

Come to think of it, writing plays all by oneself is — so lonely. I guess I have always wanted someone to write plays with. . . . I think I'm beginning to . . .

JULIE

. . . fall in love with me?

JEAN

See? What did I tell you? That's all they think about! Love and sex, sex and love!

STRINDBERG

Oh, shut up! It's always new in the hands of a genius!
(To JULIE.)
Are you — beginning to fall in love with me?

JULIE

We shall start by liking each other first, and then we shall see.

>   (JULIE and STRINDBERG stand very close together,
>   gazing into one another's eyes — THEIR sexual
>   chemistry immediately resurgent.)

JEAN

I should remind you . . .
>   (As JEAN is speaking, JULIE and STRINDBERG
>   close into a frontal embrace.)
. . . that he is dead!

JULIE and STRINDBERG
>   (In unison.)

Not anymore!

>   (JULIE and STRINDBERG withdraw from
>   THEIR embrace. JULIE holds out HER hand, and
>   STRINDBERG takes it. THEY move to depart.)

JEAN

What about me? What will become of me?

JULIE

We will be going into new territory. There won't be any headwaiters. I
don't think you would fit in.

JEAN

No headwaiters?

JULIE

I'm afraid not.

JEAN

No keeping tabs?

JULIE

None to speak of.

JEAN

But what about the bottom line?

JULIE

This is it.

JEAN

That's — all there is?

JULIE

Yes, that's all.

JEAN

But how will we know who's winning and who's losing?

JULIE

It's a new game. We shall make it up as we go along.

JEAN

I was never much good at learning new games.

JULIE

Well, then. . . .

(JULIE and STRINDBERG turn to depart.)

JEAN
(Beginning to leave in the opposite direction, then
turning.)
I shall be lonely without you. . . . I don't suppose you'll be needing any
actors.

JULIE

Oh, yes! We shall always need actors!

JEAN

I could try to learn a new part.

STRINGBERG

He does that at every performance.

JULIE

Now, no more quarrelling.
(To JEAN.)
It will have to be a very small part at first — until you get the hang of
it.

JEAN

There are no small parts, only small actors!

JULIE

Well, come along, then. But remember — the old chauvinistic bullshit
has got to go!

(JULIE and STRINDBERG again turn to depart,
JEAN now trailing them uncertainly.)

BLACKOUT

THE END

I WANT TO SHOW YOU SOMETHING

A One-Act Drama

by

Jan Henson Dow

PRODUCTION NOTES

CAST OF CHARACTERS

Dr. Fisher — 45 to 55, psychiatrist, wears a jacket and glasses

Mrs. Spencer — 35 to 40, attractive but dresses in dull clothes as if to hide her attractiveness. She carries a large purse.

SET
Dr. Fisher's office. A desk and chair are Stage Left. One chair at Stage Right and one chair next to desk.

PROPS
A phone is on the desk.

TIME
The present.

For Wendell MacNeal, who inspired me.

I WANT TO SHOW YOU SOMETHING

(DR. FISHER is seated at the desk, examining a folder.)

DR. FISHER
(HE speaks into his phone.)
Mrs. Phelps, please send in my next patient.
(Carrying the folder, HE crosses to the door at Stage Right.)

(MRS. SPENCER enters at Stage Right. SHE hesitates.)

DR. FISHER
Mrs. Spencer? I'm Dr. Fisher.

(HE offers his hand.)

MRS. SPENCER
Yes.
(Slowly, SHE shakes his hand. SHE seems to be afraid to enter.)

DR. FISHER
Won't you come in?

MRS. SPENCER
Thank you.

DR. FISHER

Please have a seat.
(HE indicates the chair at Stage Right.)

(Clutching the purse in HER hands, SHE sits on the edge of the chair.)

(HE sits behind his desk in a position that separates him from his patient.)

MRS. SPENCER

I . . . I want to thank you for seeing me so soon.

DR. FISHER

I am happy that there was an opening.
(HE studies the folder on his desk.)
I have had a chance to study your folder.

MRS. SPENCER

I filled out the form that your receptionist gave me.

DR. FISHER

She said you seemed in some distress.

MRS. SPENCER

Distress? Did she say that?

DR. FISHER

Yes.

MRS. SPENCER

I don't know if I would call it "distress".

DR. FISHER

No? What would you call it?

MRS. SPENCER

It's just that. . . . I know you must be very busy. You have a busy practice.

DR. FISHER

Yes, I do manage to keep busy.

MRS. SPENCER

I didn't want to bother you.

DR. FISHER

You haven't bothered me.   •

MRS. SPENCER

Yes, well, your time is valuable. I didn't want to disturb you.

DR. FISHER

Why would you disturb me?

MRS. SPENCER

"Disturb?" Did I say that?

DR. FISHER

Yes. Why would you "disturb" me?

MRS. SPENCER

I didn't mean "disturb."

DR. FISHER

What did you mean?

MRS. SPENCER

I . . . I . . . just . . . didn't want to abuse the privilege.

DR. FISHER

"Abuse the privilege?" Tell me about that.

MRS. SPENCER

Tell you about what?

DR. FISHER

You said, "Abuse the privilege." Tell me about that.

MRS. SPENCER

It was just an expression. It didn't mean anything.
                    (Very upset, SHE suddenly gets up from the chair.
                    HER purse slides to the floor.)
Oh, I don't know why I came here! I shouldn't be here! I'm sorry!
                    (SHE turns away toward the door.)

DR. FISHER

                    (HE gets up from his chair. Crossing around the desk,
                    HE picks up the purse.)
You dropped your purse.
                    (HE puts his hand on HER shoulder and she flinches
                    from the touch.)
There's nothing to be sorry about. Won't you sit down and tell me
what's bothering you?

MRS. SPENCER

There's nothing bothering me. I've got to go. I don't know why I
came.

DR. FISHER

Yes, you do know why you came. Please sit down.
                    (SHE sits down. HE places the purse by her chair and
                    returns to his chair behind the desk.)
Tell me why you came to see me.

MRS. SPENCER

Sometimes the mind plays tricks — the same thought, over and over
again, over and over again. If you keep thinking the same thought and
you can't stop, does that mean you're losing your mind?

DR. FISHER

What is the thought you keep thinking?

MRS. SPENCER

I didn't mean I was thinking anything.

DR. FISHER

What were you thinking?

MRS. SPENCER

Oh, God, I've got to tell someone!
        (SHE buries her face in her hands.)

DR. FISHER

It's all right. You can tell me.

MRS. SPENCER

Do you think — do you think it's a sin to kill yourself?

DR. FISHER

(HE gets up and moves around the desk. He picks up
the chair by the desk and moves it opposite her chair.
HE sits in the chair.)
Is that what you've been thinking: of killing yourself?

MRS. SPENCER

No! — Yes, I have thought about killing myself.

DR. FISHER

Do you want to tell me about that?

MRS. SPENCER

There's nothing to tell. It's just a thought.

DR. FISHER

Have you tried to kill yourself?

MRS. SPENCER

Oh, no! It's just a thought. I would never do that! I wouldn't know how to kill myself!

DR. FISHER

Well, there are many ways. Have you ever imagined hurting yourself?

MRS. SPENCER

No! I would never. . . .

DR. FISHER

Never what?

MRS. SPENCER
(Very upset, SHE stands.)

I don't know why I came. I've got to go! I've got to get out of here!
(SHE turns toward the door. HER shoulders sag in despair.)

Oh, God! I've got to tell someone! I've got to tell someone!

DR. FISHER
(Stands and gently leads her back to the chair.)

Yes, you can tell me.

MRS. SPENCER
(Turns back and slowly sits down. Long Pause.)

Do you know the play *Our Town* by Thornton Wilder?

DR. FISHER
(HE sits down.)

Our Town? Yes, I do know the play.

MRS. SPENCER

It's set in a small town in New England. I came from a small town in New England.

DR. FISHER

Did you?

MRS. SPENCER

Yes.

DR. FISHER

Was it like the one in the play?

MRS. SPENCER

No. It wasn't called Grover's Corners. It wasn't at all like Thornton
Wilder's small town.

DR. FISHER

What was it like?

MRS. SPENCER

In his town, everything was all sweetness and light. No one ever did
anything wrong . . . anything bad. Everyone was kind to each other.

DR. FISHER

Your town wasn't like Thornton Wilder's small town?

MRS. SPENCER

No. It wasn't like his small town.

DR. FISHER

How was it different?

MRS. SPENCER

He lied.

DR. FISHER

How did he lie?

MRS. SPENCER

He didn't show the darkness under all the sweetness and light.

DR. FISHER

Tell me about the darkness.

MRS. SPENCER
(Intensely)

If I tell you, you must promise not to tell anyone what I said. You must promise!

DR. FISHER

Unless it concerns potential child abuse or harming yourself or another. . . .

MRS. SPENCER
(SHE stands.)

No! Put your hand on your heart and say, "I promise. Cross my heart and hope to die."

(SHE crosses her heart and holds up her right hand.)

DR. FISHER
(HE stands and puts his hand on his heart.)

I promise.
(HE crosses his heart and holds up his right hand.)

Cross my heart and hope to die. Now, tell me about your small town.
(HE sits down. SHE remains standing.)

MRS. SPENCER

In our town there was a youth choir, like the one in Thornton Wilder's play.

DR. FISHER

Did you sing in the choir?

MRS. SPENCER

My mother said, "You have a lovely voice, just like I had when I was your age. You should sing in the choir. Would you like to join?" And I said, "Yes."

(Each time SHE says, "Yes," there is anguish underneath the "Yes.")

DR. FISHER

How old were you?

MRS. SPENCER

I was eight years old. At first, I was afraid to sing. But the choir master — like the one in Thornton Wilder's play — he encouraged me to sing.

(SHE moves to Stage Right area.)

He said, "You have a lovely voice. I'm going to tell your mother that your voice could be developed. Would you like that?"

(In anguish)

And I said, "Yes."

DR. FISHER

Did he speak to your mother?

MRS. SPENCER

Yes. He told her . . . he would be willing to give me special lessons after choir practice to . . . help me develop my voice.

DR. FISHER

What did your mother say?

MRS. SPENCER

Mother said, "We don't have money to pay for special lessons."

(SHE is obviously in distress.)

DR. FISHER

What happened then?

MRS. SPENCER

He said, "It's all right. It will be — my pleasure to give her lessons, to help her develop her voice." And so mother said it was all right.

DR. FISHER

That was very generous of him.

MRS. SPENCER
(Very upset)
Generous? Generous? I wouldn't call it generous!

DR. FISHER
What would you call it?

MRS. SPENCER
(Very upset)
I'd call it — I'd call it — I don't know what I'd call it!
(SHE sits down.)

DR. FISHER
What happened after you joined the choir?

MRS. SPENCER
(SHE stands and moves to the Stage Right area.)
One day he told me to stay after choir practice when everyone else
went home. At first — he showed me how to breathe — from the
abdomen. He said, "Stand up straight."
(SHE stands up straight.)
He said, "Relax your shoulders," and he put his hands on my shoulders
and rubbed my back."Doesn't that feel good?" he said.

And I said, "Yes."

"Breathe in and fill your tummy with air," he said, and he put his hands
on my tummy. And I breathed in.

"No, like this," he said and he put my hands on his tummy and we
breathed in together. In and out. In and out. "That's very good," he
said. "You're doing exactly what I want you to do."

DR. FISHER
How did that make you feel?

MRS. SPENCER

At first, I felt proud that he was paying so much attention to me.

DR. FISHER

Did you tell your mother about the breathing lesson?

MRS. SPENCER

When I got home, Mother said, "How was the lesson?"
(SHE sits down.)
"It was good," I said. "He's teaching me how to breathe."

"Well, it's very kind of him to take all this time. You mind him, now, and do exactly what he says."

And I said, "Yes."
(SHE gets up, very upset, and turns away.)
Oh, I don't know how to tell you what happened next. I'm . . . I'm so . . . so ashamed!

DR. FISHER

It's all right. Just tell me in your own words.

MRS. SPENCER

One day after choir practice, he called me into his office behind the choir.
(SHE stands, enacting at Stage Right what had happened.)
"I want to show you something," he said.

I thought he wanted to show me something more about breathing. I followed him into his office, and he closed the door and turned the lock.

"Take off your blouse," he said.

I was ashamed to take off my blouse.

"Don't be silly," he said. "Here, I'll help you." And he unbuttoned my blouse
    (SHE mimes unbuttoning her blouse.)

"Breathe in," he said," like this" and he put his hands on — my shoulders and then slowly down my chest. "Just relax," he said.

"Like this?" I asked. I wanted to please him.

"No, like this," he said and he unbuttoned his shirt and he took my hands and put them on his chest and slowly rubbed his chest with my hands.

"Now like this," he said and he held my hands and put them on his tummy and held them there while he unzipped his pants.

    (SHE paces back and forth, very agitated.)

Oh, I knew what he did was wrong. I was shaking all over, but I was too afraid to call out. I was afraid someone would see what we did. I was afraid someone would find out.

When it was over, he said, "Put on your blouse."

And I did what he told me.

Then he opened a drawer in his desk and pulled out a gun.
    (SHE mimes opening a drawer and pulling out a gun
    and pointing it.)

He pointed it at me.

"This gun is loaded," he said. "If you ever tell anyone, I'll kill you, and I'll kill your parents."

I was so afraid.

"Now, go on home and don't say a word to anyone about what happened."
>   (Very dejected, SHE crosses to the chair.)
And I went home.
>   (SHE sits down.)

DR. FISHER

How often did this happen?

MRS. SPENCER

Every week after choir practice, he would say, "I want to show you something."

And I knew what would happen.
>   (SHE stands and looks out into the distance as if in a
>   dream.)
But I began to have the strangest feeling like — I wasn't really there, like I was standing outside myself — watching — myself as if I'm a character in a play. I feel that way now.

DR. FISHER

How do you feel?

MRS. SPENCER

That I'm a character in a play, and I'm watching myself act a part. I'm not really here.

DR. FISHER

Did you ever tell anyone what happened?

MRS. SPENCER

No. I was afraid if people found out what we did, they would think it was my fault! They would blame me for what happened! That it was my fault! It was my fault!

DR. FISHER

Did you ever try to tell your parents?

MRS. SPENCER

I was afraid to tell my father. I didn't know what he would do. I tried to tell my mother once,

(Very upset.)

"I don't want to go to choir practice anymore. I hate it!"

And she said, "Not go to choir practice? Who ever heard of such a thing? Why you have a lovely voice."

"No! I don't want to go anymore!"

"Why what's come over you?" she said. "Now, I don't want to hear another word out of you. Why what would people say if they found out?"

And I thought, "What would people say if they found out?"

And so I went to choir practice. Week after week, he would call me into his office after everyone else had left. "I want to show you something," he would say.

DR. FISHER

How long did this go on?

MRS. SPENCER

Until I was twelve.

(Very agitated SHE crosses to the chair and sits down.)

One morning after I turned twelve, my mother woke me up.

"Come downstairs,." she said. "I want to show you something."

I was afraid to go downstairs. I was afraid of what she would say.

"There's been some shocking news."

She showed me the morning paper. In big headlines it said, "Choir Master Found Dead."

My father read from the article. "Choir master found dead. Shot by his own gun. The police suspect it was a suicide. His wife said he had a history of drinking and depression."

My father looked at me in a strange way. "At choir practice, did he ever seem to be drinking?"

"No," I said.

"Of course, there were rumors about his drinking," my mother said. "I'm so sorry," she said." He was a good man."

That day at school, everyone was talking about his death.

DR. FISHER

Did anyone ever question you?

MRS. SPENCER

(Obviously agitated, SHE stands.)

The next day the sheriff came to the principal's office. He called the choir members into the office. He asked us if we had seen anything. We all said we had left together. The death was finally declared a suicide. I thought that would be the end of it. I thought he would never bother me again.

DR. FISHER

But it wasn't the end?

MRS. SPENCER

(Very upset)

No, it wasn't the end! It will never end! Never! There hasn't been a day that I haven't felt guilty about what happened!

DR. FISHER

Yes, I understand.

MRS. SPENCER

No! You don't understand! No one could understand! I didn't feel guilty because he was dead! I hated him! I hated him! I was glad he was dead!

DR. FISHER

Then why do you feel guilty?

MRS. SPENCER

For what he made me do! For what we did together!

DR. FISHER

What he did to you wasn't your fault. You were only a child.

MRS. SPENCER

No! No! You don't understand! It was my fault! It was my fault! I can never forgive myself! Never! You don't know what happened!

DR. FISHER

Tell me what happened.

MRS. SPENCER

One day Emily, who was eight, joined the choir. I saw the way he looked at her. I knew. . . .

DR. FISHER

What did you know?

MRS. SPENCER

I knew one day he would say to her, "I want to show you something."

I couldn't let that happen.

DR. FISHER

Did you try to warn someone?

MRS. SPENCER

No! You don't understand! No one would understand! I couldn't tell anyone! What would they think?

DR. FISHER

What did you do?

MRS. SPENCER

One day after choir practice, I heard him say to Emily, "You have a lovely voice. Tell your mother I would like to give you special lessons."

When Emily left, her face was glowing. She seemed so happy.

"He wants to give me special lessons, too," she said.

> (SHE enacts at Stage Right the scene with the choir master. SHE crosses to Stage Right.)

It was then that I went into his office and got the gun where he kept it in his desk.

After everyone had left, I called to him.

"Come here", I said. "I want to show you something."

I saw the way he smiled when he came in the door. But he stopped smiling when I raised the gun.

> (SHE lifts both arms as if holding a gun at arms' length. SHE points the gun at Dr. Fisher. HE stands. HER whole body is shaking.)

MRS. SPENCER and DR. FISHER

No!

MRS. SPENCER

He shouted, and he turned his head, and I fired.

He fell to the floor. There was blood everywhere. I knew he was dead.

And I thought, "What will people think if they find out? They'll know — everything that happened."

I kneeled by his body.

> (SHE kneels on the floor as if in prayer. Pause, as if SHE is trying to decide what to do.)

I picked up the gun and I wiped the handle, and put it in his outstretched hand.

> (SHE stands up.)

And then I ran home.

> (SHE crosses to the chair.)

I got into bed and pulled the covers over my head.

> (SHE sits down and bows her head as if she is pulling the covers over her head. Finally, SHE looks up.)

When my mother came to my room, she said, "What's the matter?"

"I don't feel well," I said. "My tummy hurts."

She put her hand on my forehead." You don't have a fever. Just rest, and later I'll make you some nice chicken soup. That will make you feel better."

All night my body was shaking and I hurt all over. I was afraid when they found him they would find out what I did! That it was my fault! It was my fault!

DR. FISHER

That you killed him?

MRS. SPENCER
(SHE stands as if confronting DR. FISHER.)
No! You still don't understand! You just don't understand!

DR. FISHER
(HE stands.)
Tell me.

MRS. SPENCER
Don't you see? I was afraid everyone would find out what we did to each other. Don't you see? I hated him! I hated him!
(SHE slowly moves toward him and places her hands on his chest, slowly rubbing her hands down his chest.)
But — I began — slowly — to like what he did to me. I began to like it.
(SHE turns away.)
And then, when Emily came, I was afraid she would take my place. It was then I killed him.

(THEY are facing each other at Down Center Stage.)

I will never forgive myself! Never! I will never forgive myself for anything I did! Now do you understand?

(DR. FISHER is silent.)

MRS. SPENCER
It doesn't matter. I warned you — no one would understand. But I had to tell someone, and now I've told you. Now, it's your secret, too.

(Pause. SHE seems harsh and dominate.)

Remember, you promised not to tell anyone what I did? You won't tell, will you?
(SHE crosses her heart.)
Cross your heart and hope to die.
(SHE raises her right hand.)

(DR. FISHER is stunned. HE slowly sits down and slumps forward. SHE looks down at him.)

SLOW FADE TO BLACK

THE END

PATROL

A One-Act Drama

by

Jan Henson Dow
and
Robert Schroeder

PRODUCTION NOTES

CAST OF CHARACTERS
(In order of appearance)

Private Freeman — Male, early 20s, three-year enlisted man

Corporal Davis — Male, early 20s, well-built, muscular, career Regular Army

Corporal McCoy — Female, early 20s, Communications Specialist, reservist called to active duty

Sergeant Perry — Male, early 30s, sturdy, career Regular Army

Private Billy Pierson — Male, 18 years old, recently enlisted, no military career intentions

Davis' Father — An older man dressed in faded overalls and a slouch hat. (Actor playing Freeman doubles as Davis' Father.)

TIME AND PLACE
The present. A stark desert landscape.

THE SET
An unrealistic setting suggests an ominous desert landscape. At stage

left, an improvised camouflaged awning provides the only protection from the yellow-orange glare of a desert sun.

There is an indication that the patrol's Humvee vehicle is parked off-stage left.

Upstage right, a dune rises from the barren expanse.

COSTUMING
Mottled desert-blending Army fatigues with appropriate insignia.

PROPS
Currently-utilized Army weapons and gear.

For my grandsons: Brendan and Ian.

PATROL

(It is early in the morning. PVT. FREEMAN is standing guard Down Right, holding his rifle across his chest. CPL. DAVIS enters Down Left, followed by CPL. MCCOY. Neither carries weapons.)

MCCOY

Well?

DAVIS

Well, what?

MCCOY

Did you fix it?

DAVIS

Did I fix it? Hell, no! I can't fix it.

MCCOY

What do you mean you can't fix it?

DAVIS

That fucker ain't got no spark plugs.

MCCOY

What do you mean it doesn't have any spark plugs? It's got to have spark plugs! It got us here!

DAVIS
Man, I'm tellin' you. It ain't got no plugs!

MCCOY
We drove here in that Humvee! What are you telling me, "It ain't got no plugs?"

DAVIS
Man, you are a quick learner. I can see why you call yourself a "Communications Expert."

MCCOY
And I can see why you call yourself a mechanic.

DAVIS
I don't call myself nothing! I am the best goddamn mechanic in this here goddamn company! And I'm tellin' you that Humvee ain't got no plugs! And it ain't got no PCV valve! And it ain't got no ignition harness! Now you communicate with that!

MCCOY
Out here in nowhere, don't give me this shit!

DAVIS
Baby, I ain't givin' you nothin'.

(PVT FREEMAN has been trying his best to concentrate on his lookout task, but has not been able to help responding to what he has been hearing with growing concern.)

MCCOY
Are you saying the enemy came in here last night and stripped that vehicle right under our noses?

FREEMAN

No one came by here! No, sir! Not while I'm on guard! Maybe Davis saw something on his turn — but I didn't!

MCCOY

Or maybe Davis knows something he's not telling.

DAVIS

(To FREEMAN)

Why don't you ask McCoy here what she saw and maybe isn't telling? It was her turn after me. Everything has hooo-ah when I went off duty. I don't know nothin' 'bout missing plugs and a missing PCV valve and a missing harness!

MCCOY

I saw nothing and heard nothing. And I believe Freeman when he says he saw nothing and heard nothing. . . . What's coming down, Davis? You're the only one of us who knows where to look for a PCV valve or even what it looks like!

FREEMAN

Yeah! And what's a Humvee doin' with some kind o' harness? We ain't no fuckin' cavalry!

MCCOY

And if some spark plugs are missing, why aren't there some spares in the toolbox? Well, Corporal Best Goddamn Mechanic?

DAVIS

(To MCCOY)

If you was a real soldier, I'd. . . .

MCCOY

If you're a real mechanic you'll get that Humvee going! I don't care whether you fucked that vehicle up or who did — it's your job to fix it! How in the hell are we going to get out of here if you can't fix the goddamn Humvee? Fix it! That's your job!

DAVIS

You're the "Communications Expert," Army Reserve twice-a-month
style! You tell me how I'm s'posed to fix something that ain't got all its
parts. Communicate, Corporal! Communicate! That's your job!

MCCOY

I'm communicating! Work on that vehicle! Work, Corporal! Work!
That's your job!

DAVIS

Man, you got to have the parts. You know what I mean? You got all
your parts, you goin' to see some action. You got only a hole where
your parts s'posed to be, you get screwed. Know what I mean?

MCCOY

Davis, you've got a hole where your brains are supposed to be! Know
what I mean?

FREEMAN

Look out! Sarge comin' over the hill.

(SGT. PERRY enters Up Right, carrying PVT.
PIERSON over his shoulder. Two rifles are slung from
HIS other shoulder. PERRY descends the dune slope as
HE approaches the OTHERS, then places PIERSON
on the ground Down Center.)

PERRY

Davis, put these in the tent.

(HE hands the rifles to DAVIS, who crosses to the
awning where HE deposits the rifles.)

McCoy, give me your canteen.

(MCCOY hands PERRY HER canteen, and PERRY
dabs water on PIERSON'S face. PIERSON stirs, then

begins to come to. As HE does, PERRY holds the canteen to PIERSON'S lips. PIERSON drinks, coughs, then as consciousness returns, becomes suddenly panicky and struggles to rise.)

PIERSON

Let me go! I've got to go!

PERRY
(As HE restrains PIERSON.)
It's all right, Pierson! Just — relax!

PIERSON

I saw her! I tell you, I saw her! Let me go! I've got to go!

PERRY

You've had too much sun. Just rest. You'll be all right.

PIERSON

You don't believe me!
(To FREEMAN.)
I tell you, I saw her!

FREEMAN

What was it, Billy?

PERRY

It was just a — mirage. He needs to rest.

PIERSON
(Scanning the OTHERS as HE speaks, searching for a sign that someone is believing HIM.)
She was standing in the doorway. She was callin' me to come home to supper.

MCCOY

Who was calling you?

DAVIS

He just got too much sun.

PIERSON

You don't believe me!

(HE resumes HIS struggle to get up. Again, PERRY
restrains HIM.)

MCCOY
(Kneeling, holding the canteen to PIERSON'S lips.)
It's all right, Billy.

DAVIS

You just got too much sun, that's all.

(PIERSON pretends to relax as MCCOY continues
to kneel beside HIM, comforting HIM. PERRY
rises, believing the situation to be in hand. Suddenly
PIERSON dashes the canteen out of MCCOY'S hand,
jumps up, and crosses to Down Right, where HE stands
defiantly facing the others.)

PIERSON

You don't believe me! You think I'm crazy! I tell you, I saw my street
and the house where I was born. My mother was standing there, in the
doorway. She had a glass of water in her hand. She was callin' me to
come home to supper.
                (With a faraway look.)
"Billy! Billy! It's time for supper! Time to come home to supper."
                (Now imploringly.)
Don't you see? I've got to go. She's calling me.
                (HE turns to look over the slope of the dune, and
                beyond, and now speaks with certainty.)
It's time for supper. I've got to go home.
                (PIERSON starts up the hill, but PERRY and DAVIS
                quickly run after HIM.)

PIERSON
(As HE is being dragged.)
No. . . ! No. . . ! No . . . !

PERRY
We've got to get him back under that canvas, out of the sun!
(PERRY and DAVIS place PIERSON on the ground
under the shelter of the awning.)
Lie still, Pierson. Rest. You'll be all right. Too much sun. Just rest.

MCCOY
It's all right, Billy. You'll be all right.

PERRY
Freeman, watch him. Don't let him out of this tent!

PIERSON
You believe me, don't you, Freeman?

FREEMAN
(Kneeling beside PIERSON.)
Sure. That sun gets to you, that's all. Try to get some sleep.

DAVIS
What happened, Sarge?

PERRY
We were on our way back when Pierson suddenly ODed. He said he
saw the street where he lives, his house, his mother standing in the
doorway. He said she was — calling him to come home for supper.

MCCOY
His mother — calling him?

PERRY
Out there — you see all kinds of things not real — heat waves
shimmering out there in the desert. Just a mirage. That's all.

DAVIS

He's just a kid.

MCCOY

First time away from home. You get scared.

PERRY

He tried to run. I had to chase him — knock him out. He's just had too much sun. That's all. Just too much sun. He'll be all right once we get back to base.

DAVIS

That's just it, Sarge. We ain't getting' back to base. Not in that Humvee over there.

PERRY

What do you mean — not in that Humvee?

DAVIS

I can't fix it. I tried, but. . . .

PERRY

You can't fix it! You "tried!" What in the hell are you tellin' me?

DAVIS

I'm tellin' you the enemy must o' snuck in here last night when we was sleepin'. That Humvee's been stripped. The plugs are gone. The PVC valve gone. The ignition harness gone. It's all gone! That Humvee ain't goin' nowhere.

PERRY

Corporal, if this is some kind of joke. . . .

DAVIS

I ain't laughin', Sarge. Go see for yourself if you don't believe me.

(PERRY exits Down Left, followed by DAVIS.)

MCCOY

How is Billy?

FREEMAN

(Crossing downstage.)

He's asleep.

MCCOY

Freeman, what's going on here?

FREEMAN

Got me. I don't know what's comin' down.

MCCOY

When you were standing guard last night, did you hear or see anything — strange?

FREEMAN

Nothing'. It was . . . it was . . . spooky, though. Like it was — one of those dreams where you don't know if you're awake or not. Man! It was — quiet! I didn't hear — nothin'!

(PERRY and DAVIS enter Down Left.)

PERRY

Corporal McCoy, send a message to base. Our Humvee's disabled. We'll keep radio contact until they can send a patrol to pick us up.

MCCOY

Roger, willco.

(SHE exits Down Left.)

PERRY

Freeman, did you hear anything last night?

FREEMAN

Nothin', Sarge. There was no — sound. No sound at all.

PERRY

Davis, on your watch did anyone or anything come by this way?

DAVIS

No, Sarge, nothin'.

FREEMAN

No one got by me.

PERRY

How is Pierson?

FREEMAN

He's asleep.

PERRY

Freeman, on the alert. Don't challenge — just shoot!

FREEMAN

I ain't waitin' on nothin'.
                    (HE resumes standing guard Down Right, rifle at
                    ready.)

MCCOY
                    (Entering Down Left, deeply troubled.)
Sergeant! The radio! Something's wrong! It's — it's not working!

PERRY

Not working?

MCCOY

I don't understand it. I can't make contact. Nothing gets through!

FREEMAN
                    (Not able to hide his growing concern.)
Maybe — some kind of jamming?

PERRY

McCoy, that's your fuckin' job to keep that radio working!

(PERRY hurriedly exits Down Left, MCCOY following.)

FREEMAN

Maybe some kind of. . . .

DAVIS

What in the fuck is goin' on? First that vehicle is stripped, and we don't hear nothin'. Then Pierson goes nuts seein' things that ain't there. And now — this! What in the fuck is goin' on?

FREEMAN

They say they got a secret weapon. They say they gonna use it when the time comes.

DAVIS

Who say, man? What you talkin' 'bout?

FREEMAN

The enemy! They say they got this secret weapon! Some kinda nerve gas — bi-logical or somethin'. . . .

DAVIS

Don't give me that shit! What you talkin' 'bout — nerve gas! Bi-logical! I ain't smell no nerve gas!

FREEMAN

Maybe it don't have no smell. Maybe it just — comes on you — before you know what it is. It just. . . .

DAVIS

(In rising anger.)

Don't give me that shit!

FREEMAN

Cool it, man! I ain't the enemy!

>   (During the increasing heat of FREEMAN'S and
>   DAVIS' debate, PIERSON has crawled out from under
>   the awning and stealthily made HIS way over the hill,
>   exiting Up Right, undetected. PERRY enters Down
>   Left, followed by MCCOY.)

PERRY

They've fouled up our radio. Stripped our vehicle. I don't know how those bastards got in here without us hearing them, but somehow they did. We're going to have to hike back to base.

DAVIS

Sarge, if you ask me, that's a mighty long hike.

PERRY

I'm not asking you, Corporal. I'm telling you! Pack the supplies. Only what's essential. Leave everything else. We'll move out at dusk when the heat of the day is over.

MCCOY

Sergeant — can we carry enough water?

PERRY

It will have to be enough. By now Base knows we've lost contact. They'll have sent out a search party. We'll probably meet them halfway.
>   (HE pulls out HIS compass.)
We should move out toward the southeast — I'll just take a bearing now.
>   (HE looks at the compass and then, not believing what
>   HE is seeing, shakes the compass furiously and then
>   stares at it again.)

MCCOY

What is it?

PERRY

The compass! It's not working!

MCCOY

Not working?

(PERRY hands MCCOY the compass. SHE shakes it, looks at it, then shakes it again.)

DAVIS
(Peering at the compass over MCCOY'S shoulder.)

What the fuck?!

MCCOY
(Tilting and turning the compass, checking it out in various positions)

It doesn't point anywhere.

FREEMAN

What're we gonna do without a compass?

(PERRY looks up at the sun and then at HIS watch.)

PERRY

My God!

(One by one the OTHERS look at THEIR watches.)

FREEMAN

Stopped.

DAVIS

Stopped.

MCCOY

Stopped.

(Stunned, SHE hands the compass back to PERRY.)

PERRY

It's that sand storm we came through yesterday. It fouls up everything. You lose your way. Nothing works right anymore.

DAVIS

Freeman here, he say they got a secret weapon — nerve gas — bi-logical — somethin' we don't know nothin' 'bout.

PERRY

Cut that crap!

DAVIS

But Sarge, last night — it weren't like no other night. . . . Too still. Maybe they do have a secret weapon. Make us see things that ain't there. Make us not see what is there. . . .

PERRY

It was that storm we went through yesterday. The night just seemed still — after that storm. That was — yesterday. . . . Yesterday?

(ALL are solemnly silent for several beats.)

MCCOY
(Finally.)

Sergeant — how will we get back to Base without a compass — without a radio?

DAVIS

Yeah, Sarge — how we gonna do that?

FREEMAN

Sarge. . . ?

PERRY

We'll hunker down here. Base knows we've lost contact. A search party will already be on the way. . . . In the meantime, McCoy, take that goddamn radio apart piece by piece.

FREEMAN

Sarge, suppose they don't find us?

PERRY

They'll find us. Starting now, water is going to be rationed. All of you
— stack your canteens under the canvas.

(PERRY hands HIS canteen to MCCOY. SHE collects
the canteens.)

MCCOY

(Now realizing that PIERSON is gone.)

Sergeant. . . ! Sergeant!

(PERRY and DAVIS stop, and turn to face MCCOY)

Pierson! Gone!

(PERRY crosses hurriedly to the awning.)

DAVIS

Gone?

PERRY

(Staring first at the empty shelter, and then turning
furiously to FREEMAN.)

You son-of-a-bitch! I told you to watch him!

FREEMAN

I thought he was asleep.

PERRY

You thought! Private, you are not paid to think! We'll have to go after him. He
can't have gotten far. Might be just walking around in circles, shape he was in.
. . . We'll find him. Davis, stand guard. Shoot anything that moves. Freeman,
bring just one of those canteens. And remember, the rest of you, that water is
rationed. . . ! McCoy, get that radio working, or it'll be your ass!

MCCOY
(Aside to DAVIS.)
Our ass!

DAVIS
You got that right.

(After picking up one of the canteens, FREEMAN joins
PERRY and both, guns slung over THEIR shoulders,
disappear over the dune, exiting Up Right. DAVIS takes
up his guard position, Down Right, gun at ready. MCCOY
exits Down Left and reenters immediately carrying the
radio. She kneels, Down Left, and starts to take it apart.)

MCCOY
(After several beats, turning away from the radio and
staring off into the distance.)
Davis. . . .

DAVIS
Yeah?

MCCOY
What do you think is going on?

DAVIS
Wish to God I knew.

MCCOY
What do you think really happened to Pierson?

DAVIS
You got me.

MCCOY
He said he saw — his mother. She was calling him to come home. Do
you think he really heard her calling?

DAVIS

Sometimes things like that happen. Billy's just a kid. He might o' been thinkin' 'bout her.

MCCOY

Maybe. . . . If you hear voices — does that mean — maybe you're crazy?

DAVIS

Like the Sarge said, Billy got too much sun. That's all. He'll be all right.

MCCOY

Davis. . . .

DAVIS

Yeah?

MCCOY

In the storm — did we lose our way?

DAVIS

We lost somethin'. . . . Got here, is all I know.

MCCOY

Last night — when we got here — that Humvee was running all right then — wasn't it?

DAVIS

It sure as hell was. I keep that baby runnin' like we was ready for the Indy 500! Ready anytime we pull out. Man, she ready to go! When I say I'm the best goddamn mechanic in this here company, you better believe it.

MCCOY

I know you are, Davis. I'm sorry for what I said.

DAVIS

That's okay.

MCCOY

You're a good mechanic. The best.

DAVIS

You're a pretty "bad" mechanic yourself.

MCCOY

I am. But I can't fix this radio.
(SHE stands, leaving the radio of the ground.)
I don't know what's wrong with it.
(SHE looks off into the distance.)
When I joined the reserves, I didn't think I'd end up here — like this.

DAVIS

We ain't ended up yet. Don't be worryin' 'bout that.

MCCOY

I thought I'd pick up some spare bread — learn a trade — then over
and out. Maybe have a chance of getting a better job back being a full-
time civilian. After my divorce, I couldn't get any kind of job that paid
anything.

DAVIS

I know what you mean. They don't hardly give you no chance. Anyhow,
I ain't never had no choice. My daddy, he was dirt poor. Kept tryin' to
scratch a livin' outta that farm, but you can't make a livin' on a little
farm no more.

MCCOY

Is he still on the farm?

DAVIS

He died the year before I enlisted.

MCCOY

I'm sorry.

DAVIS

After my daddy died, they weren't nothin' for me down there. Only one way out for me — shoulderin' a rifle.

(There is a silence — EACH lost in remembrance.)

MCCOY
(Finally.)
Davis — sometimes I hear my children calling me.

DAVIS

You just thinkin' 'bout them — like Billy thinkin' 'bout his momma and me rememberin' my daddy.
(There is another silence, MCCOY'S look and manner now so faraway as to trigger DAVIS' concern. When HE speaks again, it is in a soft and comforting tone.)
What's your children's names?

MCCOY

Annie — she's two. And Tim — he's four.

DAVIS

Annie and Tim. Nice names.

MCCOY

You got any children?

DAVIS

None that I know about. Sarge, he ain't got no family neither. He say the Army's all the family he's got. You lucky you got two children. Who's keepin' 'em?

MCCOY

I had to leave them with my mother. She's good with the kids.

DAVIS

You lucky you got someone — to leave 'em with.

MCCOY

Annie — she's afraid of the dark. I used to sit with her until she fell asleep. . . . Tim — he tries to be a big boy, but he was afraid, too. . . . I used to be afraid of the dark.

DAVIS

I was scared o' the dark when I was a kid. Use t' think somethin'd grab my leg out from under the bed. My daddy, he say, "What you hollerin' 'bout?" He take a broom 'n sweep out all under that bed. He say, "We got 'im that time. Scared ol' Bug-a-Bear clean off! He ain't comin' 'round here no more!" My daddy – he was somethin' else.

MCCOY
(Staring into the distance.)

Did you ever notice? There's something about the desert — the colors shimmering in the haze, a mirage off on the horizon. . . . When we move toward it, it's as if we were moving under water, as if only the mirage is real, and we are moving in a kind of dream where time has slowed down or changed or — stopped.

DAVIS
(Now also gazing off into the distance.)

. . . Begin to remember things you ain't thought about for a long time. Little things. . . . Sound of bees in the heat of summer. . . . The way the creek flowed over the rocks behind our place. The way it sparkled in the sun — cool back under the trees. I could sit there — forever — and watch the water flow. . . .

MCCOY

In the desert there's something about the light — as if after a while you are part of the light, as if you've always been part of the light and the sand and the wind, as if you're just remembering something you've — always known. . . . Listen to the wind. You can almost hear . . . something in the wind. . . .

(No longer intent upon the distance — HER eyes suddenly focusing on DAVIS.)
Davis, I have a strange feeling. . . .

DAVIS

Like — what?

MCCOY

Like — we're . . . never going to get back to Base.

DAVIS

Like the Sarge said — cut the crap!

MCCOY

You felt it, too. Last night — it was last night, wasn't it? Freeman said. . . .

DAVIS

It weren't like no night I ever saw. Like one of them — dreams where you wake up only you still dreamin'.

MCCOY

Like a dream — where you wake up . . . and you're not afraid anymore.

DAVIS

Yeah. You're not scared anymore — like it's all a dream.

(First FREEMAN and the PERRY are seen entering Up Right, then descending the dune as they cross downstage, walking single file. FREEMAN has HIS hands locked behind HIS head. PERRY follows with HIS rifle pointed at FREEMAN'S back and FREEMAN'S rifle and the canteen slung over HIS shoulder.)

PERRY

Keep your hands up! Stay away from the others!

FREEMAN

You don't understand! You've got to let me go!

PERRY

Shut up! You're under arrest, disobeying orders!

DAVIS

What the fuck is goin' on?

PERRY

Freeman tried to go AWOL.

DAVIS

AWOL? Hell, where's he goin' AWOL to in this desert?

PERRY

He was trying to take off, same as Pierson.

MCCOY

Where is Billy?

PERRY

We couldn't find him. We couldn't find — anything. Not even his tracks. . . . Corporal Davis, get those POW cuffs. Put them on Freeman here. That's an order!

DAVIS

Sarge, you know Freeman. He ain't the kind to go AWOL.

PERRY

When that Humvee was stripped, Freeman claimed he hadn't heard anything. He was the last on guard duty, right after Billy. He should have heard something, seen something — unless he was the one that stripped that vehicle.

DAVIS

Hell! Why would he? Freeman's stranded same as we are. It don't make no sense.

PERRY

I said get those cuffs! That's an order!

DAVIS

Yes, sir, Sergeant! You're the Sergeant, Sergeant!
(Making no attempt to conceal HIS reluctance, DAVIS crosses and exits Down Left.)

MCCOY

Sergeant Perry, we're in enough trouble without fighting among ourselves! Freeman, what happened out there?

DAVIS

(Reentering, carrying handcuffs and HIS rifle.)
Which one is crazy? That's what I'm wonderin'. Sarge, you go out there 'n come back with Billy slung over your shoulder like a sack o' meal. Some crazy story about a mirage! Now it's you pointin' a gun at Freeman 'n wanting me to handcuff him!

PERRY

Corporal Davis. . . !

DAVIS

Freeman ain't never done you no harm! He jump to whenever you sound off! How in the hell do you think we got wherever the hell we are? We all jump to whenever you open your mouth!

PERRY

Corporal Davis, I'm warning you! You better shut your mouth while you still can!

DAVIS
I'll shut my mouth when I hear from Freeman. I got to hear it from him. Freeman, what happened out there?

FREEMAN
It — it ain't what you're thinkin'. It ain't what any of you are thinkin'.
. . .
>   (HIS stance and manner of speaking suggest that HE is
>   seeing what HE is telling of as HE tells it.)

We were out there lookin' for Billy. Couldn't find no tracks. Nothin'. Like he — ain't never been here at all.
>   (HE pauses, as if to bring it all into brighter focus.)

I was lookin' out there — far out. At a dust devil — movin' slow like — back and forth — back and forth. Comin' closer — kickin' up dust, sun beatin' down. . . . Hard to see squintin' into that sun. Man it was bright – like pieces of broken glass made out of light. . . . Dust and the sun – hard to see. . . .
>   (HE pauses again, as if to see it all the better.)

I close my eyes, and when I open them, I was — home. Like it was an early mornin' — I could hear the birds outside the window, just waking up. My wife, she was lyin' there in bed. She was nursin' our new baby son. She smiles that warm, easy smile and holds him out to me. "This here's your newborn son," she says. And I just — reachin' out to take him — she smilin', waitin' for me to take him and hold him in my arms.
>   (Desperately turning to PERRY.)

You don't understand. I got to go on out there. They waitin' for me!
>   (FREEMAN turns, and as if sleepwalking, crosses
>   toward the top of the dune, Up Right.)

PERRY
>   (Raising HIS rifle and pointing it at FREEMAN.)

Private Freeman! Halt! Halt, or I'll shoot!

DAVIS
>   (Raising his rifle and pointing it at PERRY.)

Sergeant! You ain't shootin' nobody in the back!

(Holding HIS rifle at ready, PERRY spins around to
face DAVIS. For several beats, PERRY and DAVIS
stare intently at each other, as FREEMAN, not altering
HIS sleepwalking gait, completes HIS exit Up Right.)

PERRY
(Lowering his rifle.)
Are you going to let him die out there? I took the canteen. He doesn't
have any water. There's nowhere for him to go. . . . Davis, I'm going
to go after him and bring him back. If you're going to shoot me, you
better do it now — or you'll have to shoot me in the back.
(THEY face off for a moment longer, then DAVIS
lowers HIS rifle.)
I don't know what's going on out there, but I'm sure as hell going to
find out.
(PERRY'S eyes study DAVIS and then MCCOY.)
McCoy, you better come with me. Corporal Davis, stand guard. If
you're attacked, we'll hear the rifle. . . . McCoy, get your rifle and one
of those canteens. Follow me.

MCCOY
Sergeant — you don't understand. They've — gone. I . . . I don't think
we'll ever — find them again.

PERRY
My job is to bring this patrol back to base, and God willing, I'm going
to do just that.

(MCCOY picks up a canteen and HER rifle, and
follows PERRY up the slope of the dune. THEY exit
Up Right. DAVIS has taken up HIS guard position
Down Left. The lighting DIMS, indicating the passage
of time. Silently, DAVIS' FATHER enters Down Right,
HIS old slouch hat partly obscuring HIS features in
shadow.)

(DAVIS has been intently scanning the desert expanse.

HE suddenly stiffens as he senses the figure Down
Right. HE quickly turns and raises HIS rifle, ready to
fire.)

DAVIS

Halt! Who goes there? Halt, or I'll shoot!
                (DAVIS' FATHER does not move. Confused, DAVIS
                lowers HIS rifle, and studies the figure.)
Keep your hands where I can see them!

                (DAVIS' FATHER continues to stand silently and still,
                HIS hands held slightly apart from HIS body. DAVIS
                strains to identify the figure.)

It's getting' dark. I can't see — who it is.

DAVIS' FATHER
                (Moving toward DAVIS a step or two.)
Son. . . .

DAVIS

Daddy. . . ?

DAVIS' FATHER
I've been waiting' for you, Son.

DAVIS
                (Incredulously.)
Daddy — is it you?

DAVIS' FATHER
Plantin's all done. Just a good spring rain, and this old earth goin' to —
blossom. Everything goin' t' turn green 'n bloom again.
                (HE kneels as if sifting the earth through HIS fingers.)
Like the smell of the good earth in the early spring. You can tell by the
feel of her it's goin' t' be a bountiful harvest. Seed already planted in her
brown earth. When the spring come, her belly goin' t' ripen. . . .

(HE rises and looks into the distance.)
. . . and far as the eye can see, everything's goin' t' turn green and bloom again. After the spring come, it will be a bountiful harvest.
(Turning now to DAVIS.)
Don't worry, son. You gonna be there.

DAVIS
(Standing transfixed.)
Daddy. . . ! Daddy!

DAVIS' FATHER
It's all right. . . . You done a good job. . . . Time to come home now. They goin' t' plant you in the good earth 'n every spring you gonna grow young 'n green again, and outta your heart will blossom a tree of life.

(DAVIS lets HIS rifle fall to the ground. HE slowly crosses to the figure of HIS FATHER. DAVIS' FATHER stands silently, awaiting DAVIS' approach. When DAVIS stands before HIM, THEY look at one another for a long moment, and then DAVIS' FATHER silently puts HIS arm across DAVIS' shoulder, and THEY silently exit Down Right. After several beats, PERRY enters Up Right, followed by MCCOY.)

PERRY
(Aware at once of Davis' absence.)
Davis! Corporal Davis!
(HE crosses quickly to Down Left, where HE stands, looking all about.)
Davis!
(PERRY exits for a moment Down Left, then hurriedly crosses to exit Down Right.)
Corporal Davis!
(MCCOY does not exhibit surprise. SHE descends the dune slope slowly, then stands near stage center. PERRY reenters Down Right and crosses to MCCOY.

For a long moment, THEY look at one another.)
He's gone. . . . They're all — gone.

                    MCCOY
Sergeant — it's time to move out.

                    PERRY
I can't go without Davis — without Freeman and Pierson. They're my
responsibility.

                    MCCOY
They're not coming back. Listen. . . .

          (There is the SOUND of a rising wind.)

                    PERRY
It's only the wind.

                    MCCOY
My children are calling me. . . . Annie, she's afraid of the dark. . . .
Tim, he's just a little fella. He tries to be brave. . . . At night, when I
put them to bed, we all hold hands so they won't be scared anymore. .
. . Listen. . . .
          (Again, the SOUND of the wind.)
Annie and Tim are calling me. I've got to go.

                    PERRY
It's only the sound of the wind.

                    MCCOY
          (As SHE gazes far into the distance.)
Sergeant, the radio is — silent. All the watches — have stopped. The
compass is — dead.

                    PERRY
They've got a secret weapon.

MCCOY

There's something about the light — as if we've always been part of the light and the sand and the wind. As if we're just remembering something we've — always known.

(PERRY slowly, hesitantly, turns to look where SHE is looking — far into the distance. When HE speaks, it is an almost involuntary utterance.)

PERRY

So bright. . . ! So — white. . . ! You think you see — my God! Cliff! He caught me the time I almost pitched a no-hitter in high school! Look! He sees me! He's waving! That arm! He lost that arm when he was killed in the crash. . . ! And Pete! My God, Pete! He sees me, too, and look! He wants me to come and join them! And there's Joe — he's laughing and waving!

(HE is suddenly silent, and after a moment of concentration can be seen to force HIS eyes away from the distance by sheer power of will. Determinedly, HE focuses on MCCOY.)

I can't go without Pierson and Freeman and Davis.

MCCOY

Sergeant, it's time to move out.

PERRY

(Hesitantly. Defensively.)
D-don't you see? They're my responsibility. I can't go without them.

MCCOY

It's all right, Sergeant! It's just — time — to move out.

(MCCOY turns and starts up the hill, crossing toward Up Right.)

PERRY

McCoy! Stop! I — I can't let you do this! They're your responsibility, too.

(MCCOY stops in HER tracks and turns toward PERRY. SHE looks at HIM disarmingly, then smiles gently.)

MCCOY

Sergeant, there is a secret. . . .

PERRY

What — secret?

MCCOY

There's nothing to be afraid of anymore.
(MCCOY turns away, and is about to continue up the slope.)

PERRY

N-nothing. . . ?! All of this. . . !

(MCCOY turns back toward HIM. HE is looking at HER imploringly.)

It's — the sun. . . ! It's — the heat. . . ! It's — that stare. . . ! Like sunlight glaring off a mirror of ice!

MCCOY

Sergeant, there's nothing to be afraid of anymore.

(MCCOY turns away, and continues on HER path up the slope toward Up Right. Torn by conflicting emotions, PERRY slowly raises HIS rifle.)

PERRY

Halt!
(MCCOY does not stop. PERRY'S voice is no longer indecisive.)

Halt or I'll shoot!

(MCCOY does not stop. PERRY aims carefully at HER retreating back, then pulls the trigger. There is the SOUND of a rifle click, but there is no sound of rifle fire.)

(There is no indication that MCCOY is hit or injured. SHE exits over the hill Up Right.)

(PERRY slowly lowers HIS rifle. HE turns and stoically takes up a position Down Center. He is on guard.)

SLOW FADE to BLACK

THE END

TEN-MINUTE PLAYS

TRYING TO GET TO EUREKA

A Ten-Minute Satiric Comedy

by

Jan Henson Dow
and
Jim Pegolotti

PRODUCTION NOTES

CAST OF CHARACTERS

Tim — Middle-aged male

Male Voice Off — Announcer
Pilot
Uncle Ed

Female Voice Off — Gate Attendant
Car Rental Agent
Operator in India

SET
A chair.

For Phil Tannenholz and Steve Sosin.

TRYING TO GET TO EUREKA

VOICE OFF — MALE ANNOUNCER
Pacific Air, Flight 2323, for Eureka, California. Now departing at Gate 23. Pacific Air, Flight 2323, for Eureka. Now departing at Gate 23.

TIM
(Enters, running, carrying two large packages. Drops one of the packages. Stops to pick up the package. Shakes it to see that nothing is broken. Runs towards the gate.)

Hey, wait! Wait! Don't close that gate!

(Trying to find his ticket, he drops the second package. Stops to pick it up. Shakes it, then finds his ticket, and waving it in the air, he rushes up to the gate.)

Hey, wait! I'm supposed to be on that plane!

VOICE OFF — MALE GATE ATTENDANT
I'm sorry, Sir. Flight 2323 has just departed for Eureka.

TIM
Departed? What do you mean departed?

VOICE OFF — MALE GATE ATTENDANT
Flight 2323 has already taken off. I'm sorry, Sir.

TIM
What do you mean it's taken off? I'm supposed to be on that plane!

VOICE OFF — MALE GATE ATTENDANT
You're too late. Flight 2323 for Eureka is in the air.

TIM
What do you mean, it's in the air?

VOICE OFF — MALE GATE ATTENDANT
          (Speaking as if to a foreigner or to a small child who
          does not understand the language.)
Plane — fly. In — air. Eu — re — ka. No come back. Capish?

TIM
          (He makes a gesture of flying.)
Plane — fly. In — air. Eu — re — ka.
          (He makes a gesture of "finished.")
No come back. "Capish" this! Oh, damn! When's the next flight to
Eureka?

VOICE OFF — MALE GATE ATTENDANT
Tomorrow morning.

TIM
Tomorrow morning! But my bag is on that plane!

VOICE OFF — MALE GATE ATTENDANT
I'm sure it will be waiting for you in Eureka.

TIM
Well, I'm not in Eureka! Capish? I'm still in San Francisco, and my bag
is flying to Eureka!

VOICE OFF — MALE GATE ATTENDANT
You might inquire at Lost Luggage. I'm sure they can help you.

TIM
Lost Luggage! I don't believe this! So where's Lost Luggage?

VOICE OFF — MALE GATE ATTENDANT

Three flights down. Go to the center of the terminal, do not pass the exit. Turn left at the first escalator, and take the second escalator to the right.

TIM

Did you say turn right at the second escalator or left at. . . . Oh, to hell with it.
(He drops his packages and sits in a chair.)
And so, once again, it's a family reunion and I'm trying to get to Eureka. It's the usual "turkey" with all the trimmings. Aunts and uncles up the wazoo. Cousins I haven't seen in years. A brother I haven't spoken to since seventh grade, or he hasn't spoken to me. Something about a game where I beat the crap out of him, or he beat me. I can't remember which or why. It doesn't matter. Once again, I'm trying to get to Eureka.

My advice. Never try to fly to Eureka! It's the second foggiest airport in the world! What's the foggiest? I don't have a clue and I don't give a damn. You see, one of the main problems, the airport is built on top of a mountain. And every time you try to fly to Eureka, it's fogged in. I mean FOGGED IN! I don't mean pea soup. I mean you're walking around with a tin cup and a cane.

VOICE OFF — MALE ANNOUNCER

Pacific Air announces that Eureka is experiencing heavy fog. Flight 2323 is returning to San Francisco.

TIM

What did I tell you? FOGGED IN! This morning I flew in from La Guardia, hoping that once, just once, Eureka wasn't fogged in. And what happens? I'm not even on the plane and Eureka is fogged in!
So never try to fly to Eureka, not in the winter. And come to think of it, not in the spring, and certainly not in the fall. So that leaves the summer. But what holiday do you have in the summer? The 4th of July? You've got to be kidding! That means the high school band and a picnic

out at the park and fireworks and trying not to speak to my brother and kids getting lost and dogs barking and scratching — the whole nine yards. Eureka on the 4th? It's not exactly the Boston Tea Party. More like the Donner Party. Why do you think they went by wagon train? So they wouldn't have to fly!

VOICE OFF — MALE ANNOUNCER
Flight 2323 has landed and those who wish to disembark may disembark at San Francisco. Those who wish to try again when Eureka is no longer fogged in may reboard the plane.

TIM
Look at those dispirited people getting off the plane. Now, those deluded few who are still trying to fly to Eureka, get back on the plane, and I am one of them. I am going to get to Eureka if I have to parachute in!

VOICE OFF — MALE ANNOUNCER
The pilot has announced that parachutes will be provided.

TIM
(He climbs over other passengers to find his seat.)
Excuse me. I think that's my seat you're sitting in. After the usual "yada, yada, yada," we secure our seat belts, and, then, we sit on the tarmac for two hours. During this time, a bleary eyed attendant doles out one bag of peanuts per passenger. Amid wailing babies and starving people who have to pee, I eat my peanuts and plot my revenge.

VOICE OFF — MALE PILOT
This is your pilot speaking. We are finally cleared for takeoff.

TIM
I fall into an exhausted and troubled sleep. I am in a terrible nightmare! I dream that I am in a rocket ship aimed at Eureka. I don't know how to fly the damned thing. I push a button and eject just before. . . .
(He is startled awake.)

VOICE OFF — MALE PILOT
Because Eureka is still FOGGED IN, we will land in Medford, Oregon.

TIM
Yee, gods, Medford, Oregon! In a daze, we land in Medford, and I stagger off the plane.
>   (Carrying his packages, he staggers off the plane and
>   over to the desk.)
When is the next flight to Eureka?

VOICE OFF — MALE GATE ATTENDANT
I'm sorry, Sir. Pacific Air does not fly from Medford to Eureka. To get to Eureka, you'll have to return to San Francisco and try again.

TIM
Return to San Francisco! I can't believe this! I better call the family and let them know I'll be late. In fact, I may arrive sometime next year.
>   (Using his cell phone, he places a call.)

VOICE OFF — UNCLE ED
Hello.

TIM
Is that you, Uncle Ed?

VOICE OFF — UNCLE ED
The last time I looked, it was me. He, he, he.
>   (Very pleased with his joke.)
Who's this?

TIM
It's Tim.

VOICE OFF — UNCLE ED
>   (As if he does not know who "Tim" is.)
Tim who?

TIM

Uncle Ed, it's your nephew, Timmy.

VOICE OFF — UNCLE ED

Why didn't you say so?
(To his wife.)
Ruthie, it's your nephew, Timmy.
(To Tim.)
Your aunt says to tell you, "Hello."

TIM

Tell her, "Hello" for me.

VOICE OFF — UNCLE ED

(To his wife.)
Ruthie, he says, "Hello."
(To Tim.)
She says she's baked your favorite pie.

TIM

My favorite pie? What's that?

VOICE OFF — UNCLE ED

(To his wife.)
What kind of pie is that, Ruthie?
(To Tim.)
She's says, "Rhubarb and gooseberry."

TIM

(With thinly veiled sarcasm.)
Rhubarb and gooseberry? Tell her thanks a lot.

VOICE OFF — UNCLE ED

(To his wife.)
Ruthie, he says, "Thanks a lot." What?
(To Tim.)
She says, "Do you want us to pick you up?" Where are you?

                              TIM
Medford, Oregon.

                    VOICE OFF — UNCLE ED
Medford, Oregon? How in the hell did you get there?

                              TIM
It's a long story. The Eureka Airport is fogged in.

                    VOICE OFF — UNCLE ED
                        (To his wife.)
Ruthie, he says the Eureka Airport is fogged in.
                         (To Tim.)
She says to tell you it's the second foggiest airport in the world.

                              TIM
I've heard that one.

                    VOICE OFF — UNCLE ED
Do you want to speak to your brother?

                              TIM
Not particularly.

                    VOICE OFF — UNCLE ED
                     (To Tim's brother.)
Stanley, it's your brother, Timmy. Do you want to speak to him?
                         (Pause.)
Okeydokey.

                              TIM
What did he say?

                    VOICE OFF — UNCLE ED
He says, "No." He's still got his knickers in a knot.

TIM

Sounds like Stanley.

VOICE OFF — UNCLE ED

He says to tell you he rented a car and came in early. Better than getting
fogged in. He, he, he.

TIM
(Under his breath.)

Jerk!

VOICE OFF — UNCLE ED

What did you say?

TIM

That might work. Maybe I'll rent a car and drive on in.

VOICE OFF — UNCLE ED

Over those mountains? That's a good one!
(To those assembled to hear the exciting news.)
Did you hear that. He says he's going to rent a car and drive in over the
mountains.
(To Tim.)
Your brother says that's a dumb idea. The mountains'll be fogged in.

TIM
(Under his breath.)

Tell him to stick it up his. . . .

VOICE OFF — UNCLE ED

What did you say?

TIM

I said, "Pass. I'll try Grant's Pass."

VOICE OFF — UNCLE ED
(To Stanley.)
He says he's going to try Grant's Pass.
(To Tim.)
Stanley says, "Lots of luck."

TIM
I'll call when I get to Eureka.

VOICE OFF — UNCLE ED
Okeydokey.

(Tim hangs up.)

TIM
Next, I try to find the car rental desk. The only one is in an obscure corner of the airport behind Lost Luggage. There is a sign that says "Last Chance Rental." With not much confidence, I approach the desk.
(To the AGENT on duty.)
I'd like to rent a car. You do have a car available?

VOICE OFF — MALE CAR RENTAL AGENT
Of course, Sir. May I see your driver's license and credit card?

TIM
(Searching in his back pocket but can't find his wallet.)
I can't find my wallet! I had it right here! My driver's license, all my credit cards are in that wallet!

VOICE OFF — MALE CAR RENTAL AGENT
I'm sorry, Sir. We require a driver's license and a credit card.

TIM
You just said that! I took my wallet out of my back pocket during the flight so I wouldn't have to sit on it. I must have put it in the pocket of

the seat in front of me. I'll have to go back and find my wallet. When do you close?

VOICE OFF — MALE CAR RENTAL AGENT
In five minutes.

TIM
Five minutes! Don't close that desk! I'll be right back.
             (He rushes to the gate and speaks to the GATE AT-
             TENDANT.)
I'm in desperate trouble here! I must have left my wallet on that plane!

VOICE OFF — MALE GATE ATTENDANT
What plane was that, Sir.

TIM
You know damn good and well what plane! The one I just got off of! The one that was supposed to land in Eureka, but it couldn't because Eureka is FOGGED IN!

VOICE OFF — MALE GATE ATTENDANT
I'm sorry, Sir. That plane is just taking off for Los Angeles.

TIM
Los Angeles? Stop that plane! My wallet is on that plane!

VOICE OFF — MALE GATE ATTENDANT
You can put in a claim at the Lost and Found Desk. It's next to Lost Luggage.

TIM
You don't understand! I have no cash, no credit cards, no driver's license. They're all in my wallet which is on that plane and I'm trying to rent a car to drive to Eureka which is FOGGED IN! Stop that plane or I'm going to sue this airport! What is the name of your supervisor?

(Reaching into his inside pocket, he discovers his missing wallet.)

Oh, here it is. I guess I forgot that I put it in my inside pocket. Cancel the supervisor. I've got to get to that rental desk before it closes.

(He rushes back to the rental desk only to find that it has closed.)

I can't believe this! It's closed! Let's see what this sign says. "If the desk is closed, call this number." Good. I'll call this number.

(He gets out his cell phone and punches in the number.)

VOICE OFF — OPERATOR IN INDIA

Yes, kind Sir or Madam, may I kindly help you with your need for a conveyance?

TIM

You certainly can help me. I want to rent a car, but your desk here is closed.

VOICE OFF — OPERATOR IN INDIA

It is our pleasure for your best assistance. May I inquire, kind Sir, as to the car you wish for renting?

TIM

Any car. I don't care! You see I was trying to fly to Eureka, but Eureka is fogged in.

VOICE OFF — OPERATOR IN INDIA

So sorry for your inconvenience, Sir. Did you say "fagged in?"

TIM

No, FOGGED IN! FOGGED IN!

VOICE OFF — OPERATOR IN INDIA

Fogged In? I have never heard such as "fogged in," Kind Sir. What is its meaning, please?

TIM

It doesn't matter! I am trying to rent a car here!

VOICE OFF — OPERATOR IN INDIA

Sir, remain calm, please. We are calling for assistance of a doctor to di-
agnose your "fogged in." While we are waiting, have you ever seen the
very excellent film, *Slumdog Millionaire*?

TIM

Slumdog Millionaire!

VOICE OFF — OPERATOR IN INDIA

We are very proud of that film. Did you like the dancing and the sing-
ing at the end?

TIM

I hated *Slumdog Millionaire*! I hated the ending! I do not need a doctor!
Eureka is fogged in! FOGGED IN! Oh, forget it!
　　　(He hangs up.)

VOICE OFF — MALE ANNOUNCER

Flight 1616 now boarding for San Francisco at Gate 16. Flight 1616
now boarding for San Francisco at. . . .

TIM

San Francisco? San Francisco? Wait! Wait! Don't close that gate! I'm
coming!
　　　(He quickly exits.)

THE END

ROOM SERVICE

A Ten-Minute Comedy

by

Jan Henson Dow
and
Shannon Michal Dow

PRODUCTION NOTES

CAST OF CHARACTERS

Female Receptionist — The Sanford Hotel's receptionist. Young, perky, always polite.

Man — A hotel guest. Hung over, belligerent. Speaks with a slightly slurred voice. He is wrapped in a brightly colored table cloth and picks up a hand mirror and looks at himself and groans.

SET
Counter at Stage Left. Chairs representing a bed and bedside table at Stage Right.

They mime answering and talking on the phone.

TIME
The present.

For Sydney Dow, who inspired us.

ROOM SERVICE

(The SOUND of a phone RINGING.)

RECEPTIONIST
(Behind counter at Left. Answering the phone)
Hotel Sanford. How may I help you?

MAN
(At Right. Sits up, confused. HE is wearing a brightly
colored table cloth. He picks up a hand mirror, looks at
himself, and groans.)
What hotel is this?

RECEPTIONIST
This is the Hotel Sanford, a four-star establishment located in the heart
of downtown. . . .
(The MAN hangs up.)
Hello? Hello?
(The SOUND of a phone RINGING. Answering the
phone.)
Hotel Sanford. How may I help you?

MAN
Look, I'm trying to dial an outside number and I can't get this damn
phone to work.

RECEPTIONIST
For an outside number, dial 9.

MAN

Dial 9.

> (He hangs up and dials 9. He gets an answering
> machine.)

At the sound of the tone just stick. . . I don't want the sound of a tone. I
want Lorraine. Lorraine, pick up the damn phone. I know you're there.
Don't try to fool me. I know you, Lorraine! Lorraine! Just answer the
damn phone!

> (HE hangs up and dials the RECEPTIONIST.)

RECEPTIONIST

Hotel Sanford. How may I help you?

MAN

I want Room Service. Is this Room Service?

RECEPTIONIST

No, Sir, this is the Receptionist. I can take your order and contact
Room Service.

MAN

Good. Now listen carefully, 'cause I don' wanna have to repeat myself.
You got that?

RECEPTIONIST

Yes, Sir.

MAN

All right. I wanna lubsanwi.

RECEPTIONIST

Excuse me, Sir. I didn't quite get that.

MAN

I told you I don' wanna repeat myself.

RECEPTIONIST
Yes, Sir. But could you please say it again?

MAN
Ok. Now listen carefully. — Are ya listenin'?

RECEPTIONIST
Yes, Sir.

MAN
Good. I wanna lubsanwi.

RECEPTIONIST
Did you say you want a lubsanwi?

MAN
What kinda hotel is this? Can't a man get somethin' ta eat aroun' here?
I wanna club san-wich! Got it? A club sanwich!

RECEPTIONIST
A club sandwich. Yes, Sir.

MAN
Good. I wanna club san-wich, a bottle of whiskey, and four boxes of
matches.

RECEPTIONIST
A club sandwich, a bottle of whiskey, and four boxes of matches.

MAN
That's right. You got it.

RECEPTIONIST
Yes, Sir. There's just one problem, Sir.

MAN
What's that?

RECEPTIONIST
The hotel doesn't serve alcohol in the room at this time of day.

MAN
What do you mean you don't serve alcohol at this time of day?

RECEPTIONIST
It's 9:25 in the morning, Sir. Hotel policy prohibits any alcohol being served in the room before noon.

MAN
No alcohol until noon? What kinda hotel is this?!

RECEPTIONIST
This is the Hotel Sanford. A four star hotel located in the heart of. . . .

MAN
Shove it! I'll just come down to the bar and get a bottle.

RECEPTIONIST
The bar doesn't open until 11:00, Sir.

MAN
11:00! How in the hell am I supposed to get a drink around here?!
            (Angrily hanging up the phone. Then dialing 9.)
Lorraine — Lorraine, I know you're there. Jus' pick up the damn phone! In case you want ta know I'm at the Hotel Sanford — Room — I don't know what room. Jus' call the Receptionist. She'll put you through. Got that, Lorraine. Call the Receptionist. Hotel Sanford. We need to talk.
            (He slams down the phone and dials the receptionist.)

RECEPTIONIST
Hotel Sanford. How may I help you?

MAN
Where is the nearest liquor store?

RECEPTIONIST
Three blocks down and across the street.

MAN
Three blocks down? Is that north or south?

RECEPTIONIST
North. Is there anything else I can help you with, Sir?

MAN
Tell the bellhop to go down there, buy a bottle of whiskey, and bring it to my room.

RECEPTIONIST
I'm afraid we can't do that, Sir. It's against the rules.

MAN
Against the rules? Then jus' bring me a club sandwich.

RECEPTIONIST
There's just one more problem, Sir.

MAN
What the hell is that?

RECEPTIONIST
Club sandwiches are on our lunch menu. We don't serve club sandwiches until lunch time.

MAN
Well, then, what the hell do you serve?

RECEPTIONIST
Breakfast.

MAN
Breakfast?

RECEPTIONIST
You know — cereal, scrambled eggs, bacon, ham, grits, that kind of thing.

MAN
I know what breakfast is! Do you think I'm a dolt? Send up some scrambled eggs, a bottle of whiskey, and four boxes of matches.

RECEPTIONIST
I'm sorry, Sir, whiskey is alcohol.

MAN
Are you trying to get smart with me?

RECEPTIONIST
No, Sir.

MAN
Then just give me scrambled eggs and four boxes of matches.

RECEPTIONIST
One order of scrambled eggs and four boxes of matches coming right up. Could you give me your room number?

MAN
My room number?

RECEPTIONIST
Room Service usually delivers food to your room. That's why it's called Room Service, Sir.

MAN
Are you getting uppity with me, Missy?

RECEPTIONIST
No, Sir. But I can't send your order if I don't know what room you're in.

MAN

Jus' a minute.

> (He crosses to the door, opens it, and looks at the number.)

Now listen carefully, 'cause I don' wanna have to say this again.

RECEPTIONIST

I'm listening, Sir.

MAN

1219. Got that?

RECEPTIONIST

1219. Got it.

MAN

Cut that crap!

RECEPTIONIST

Yes, Sir.

MAN

Okay, then I want some bacon and strawberries. Do you have any strawberries?

RECEPTIONIST

Yes, Sir.

MAN

And some toast with orange marmalade and some hot coffee, and I said, "hot." You got all that?

RECEPTIONIST

Scrambled eggs, bacon, strawberries, toast with orange marmalade, and very hot coffee. There's just one problem, Sir.

MAN

No strawberries?

RECEPTIONIST

It's now 9:31. Room Service isn't available for breakfast after 9:30.

MAN

I'm losing my mind here. Send up two slices of bread, bacon, scrambled eggs, and strawberries on the side.

RECEPTIONIST

That is called a club sandwich. Club sandwiches are served at lunchtime which begins at 11:00.

MAN

Is this Hell? This is Hell, isn't it? I'm dead, and now I'm in a friggin' bedroom in Hell where I can't get a friggin' drink and I can't get any friggin' food!

RECEPTIONIST

No, this is the Hotel Sanford, a four star establishment located in the heart of. . . .

MAN

Can it. How about my four boxes of matches?

RECEPTIONIST

I'm sorry, Sir, I can't send you up four boxes of matches.

MAN

Why the hell not?

RECEPTIONIST

Your room is a non-smoking room, Sir. It's against hotel policy to send matches to a non-smoking room. We would assume anyone asking for matches would be asking for them because they want to smoke in a non-smoking room.

MAN

Suppose I don't smoke?

RECEPTIONIST

Excuse me, Sir?

MAN

I said, "Suppose I don't smoke?" Now can I have my matches?

RECEPTIONIST

If you don't mind my asking, if you don't smoke, what do you want with four boxes of matches?

MAN

That's my business.

RECEPTIONIST

Well, I'm sorry, but hotel policy stipulates that. . . .

MAN

You better send me up my matches, Missy! Or I'll burn this friggin' hotel down to the ground!

RECEPTIONIST

Sir, how can you burn the hotel down if you don't have any matches, Sir?

MAN

You're going to be sorry for that smart ass remark. I'm going to report you to the management!

RECEPTIONIST

Yes, Sir.

MAN

Now look here, Missy. I'm going to give you one more chance. When I say, "Jump!" You say, "How high?" Got that?

RECEPTIONIST

Yes, Sir. When you say, "Jump," I say, "How high?"

MAN

Now I want you to get Lorraine — Lorraine on the phone. Tell her —
tell her that I. . . .

RECEPTIONIST

To call an outside number just dial 9.

(MAN pulls out the telephone cord and throws the
phone across the room.)

Sir? Are you still there? Sir? Well, thank you for staying at the Hotel
Sanford, a four star establishment located in the heart of. . . .

BLACK OUT

THE END

THE FOURTH WALL

A Ten-Minute Satiric Comedy

by

Jan Henson Dow

PRODUCTION NOTES

CAST OF CHARACTERS

Amanda — of a certain age, playwright/director

Man — in his 30's, handsome

Woman — in her 40's, slim, good looking

Inge'nue — 18, slim, pretty

SETTING
Stage of a theatre. A few chairs are placed around the stage.

TIME
The present.

For Phil Tannenholz.

THE FOURTH WALL

(MAN, in HIS thirties, handsome. HE enters Up Right and looks around.)

                    WOMAN
(WOMAN, in HER forties, good looking. SHE enters Up Right. SHE looks around. Sees the MAN and walks toward HIM. THEY hug and air kiss.)
Good to see you. You're looking handsome, as usual!

                    MAN
Yes, I agree.

                    WOMAN
It's been forever.

                    MAN
Not since that turkey. I forget the name.

                    WOMAN
The Turkey.

                    MAN
Right. It lasted one night. The critics ripped us apart.

                    WOMAN
Well, what can you expect? Critics!

MAN

If they could act, they'd be actors.

WOMAN

Of course. Where is our director?

MAN

Not here.

WOMAN

I can see that. Were you given a script?

MAN

No. I just received a call. What's this all about?

WOMAN

I don't know. I suspect we'll find out when Amanda gets here.

(AMANDA enters from Stage Left.)

WOMAN

(Crosses to hug and air kiss Amanda.)

Amanda! So good to see you!

AMANDA

Good to see you. Glad you're on time. That's my first rule for actors.
Be on time.

WOMAN

So good of you to ask us. I'm so impressed. Your new play is selling out.

AMANDA

Interesting way to put it.

WOMAN

You know what I mean. Lights up on Broadway, critics cheering,

"Author! Author!" and all that. You've met. . . .
                    (Indicates the MAN, but does not say HIS name.)

                          AMANDA
Yes, of course. I saw you in *The Turkey*.

                           MAN
Did you? And what did you think of my performance?

                          AMANDA
                    (Beat)
Interesting.
                    (Beat)
I thought you'd like another go at stardom.
                    (Looks around.)
And where is our inge'nue? She's late.

                           MAN
We haven't seen her. Appears she's defied your first rule.

                          AMANDA
Well, we'll just get started then.

                          WOMAN
I don't have a script.

                          AMANDA
There is no script.

                           MAN
No script?

                          AMANDA
We'll improvise.

MAN

Improvise? Yee, gods!

WOMAN

I love to improvise. It awakens my inner child.

MAN
(Cynically)
Does it? That must have been a while ago.
(Beat)
I hate to improvise.

AMANDA

Then we'll see what it awakens in you. Ah, she's arrived at last.

INGE'NUE
(SHE is somewhat flustered. SHE enters from Up Right. SHE sees AMANDA and crosses and shakes hands.)
You must be our playwright.

AMANDA

Yes, you are perceptive.

INGE'NUE

I've seen your photo in *Variety*.

AMANDA

Have you?

INGE'NUE

Yes, and the *New York Times*. I'm sorry I'm late. It looked like it was going to rain. I thought I'd take the subway, but I knew I'd be late, so I had to take a taxi, but he let me off on the wrong corner. The traffic is awful. I promise to be on time for our next rehearsal. I'm. . . .

AMANDA

I know who you are. You're our inge'nue. No need for names.

INGE'NUE

Oh? Okay. My agent told me to be here at 10:00, but he didn't give me a script.

AMANDA

There is no script. We're going to improvise.

INGE'NUE

Oh, goodie! I love to improvise!

MAN

I knew you would.
            (To AMANDA as he looks around the stage.)
Our director doesn't seem to be here? He's, also, broken your first rule.

AMANDA

Not at all. I'm going to direct my own play.

MAN

A playwright directing her own play? Isn't that a bit risky? Doesn't allow for much objectivity.

AMANDA

Objectivity is highly overrated. Everything is subjective.

MAN

Everything is subjective?

AMANDA

Yes. We create our reality as we go along. In fact, as we improvise, we create our reality.

MAN

Interesting concept. I presume this play, at least, has a title, or do we improvise that as we go along?

AMANDA

No, the title is *The Fourth Wall*.

WOMAN

The Fourth Wall? What does that mean? Sounds like a political thriller.

MAN

"Mr. Gorbachev, tear down that wall!"

WOMAN

Exactly.

INGE'NUE

Who is Mr. Gorbachev?

(MAN and WOMAN look at each other.)

MAN

You have heard of Ronald Reagan?

INGE'NUE

Of course.
(Beat)
He was an actor wasn't he?

MAN

Yes.
(Beat)
He played a President.

INGE'NUE

I remember now. Didn't he get an Academy Award for that performance?

MAN

Yes, I believe he did.

WOMAN

So the title is *The Fourth Wall*? Who is the main character?

AMANDA

All of us.

WOMAN

All of us? Is this a comedy?

AMANDA

Yes, and a tragedy?

MAN

(Startled)
A comedy and a tragedy?

AMANDA

Yes. We make mistakes, do foolish things, and then drop dead at the end.

MAN

Makes sense to me. What about *The Fourth Wall*?

AMANDA

(SHE walks towards the audience and waves her hands.)
We totally demolish the fourth wall.

INGE'NUE

(Very upset, moving forward as if to stop her.)
You mustn't do that! You mustn't break the fourth wall!

AMANDA

Why not?

INGE'NUE

There's a rule against it. I learned that in Acting One. It's called "suspension of disbelief" or something like that. Maybe it's called "The Scottish Play".

(MAN and WOMAN react with shock and horror.)

WOMAN

You mustn't say that! Don't say, "The Scottish Play"!

INGE'NUE

You just said it.

WOMAN

Well, it's very bad form.

MAN

Who's going to play the villain?

AMANDA

I am.

MAN

You're going to be the playwright and the director and the main character and the villain?

AMANDA

Yes, somehow I'm always drawn to villains. They're so much more interesting.

MAN

But I always play the villain. Iago! Shylock! The Turkey!

AMANDA

Yes, it suits you.

MAN

Then, that's settled. I get to play the villain.

AMANDA

I think not.

MAN
(Very upset)
You can't play the villain! You're the playwright!

AMANDA

Yes, I am the playwright. That's why I can do anything I choose. It's in my contract.

INGE'NUE
(Very upset)
But you can't play all the parts. It destroys the illusion.

AMANDA

Destroys the illusion?

MAN

Yes, she has a point.

AMANDA

What illusion?

INGE'NUE
(SHE makes confused gestures.)
That the playwright is separate from the characters and the actors are separate from the audience. That's why there's a fourth wall. We are the actors. And you are the playwright, and they are the audience. We act out their emotions, and they watch us acting out their emotions with our own emotions, and then you write it all down. Or maybe you write it down first, I'm not quite sure. Now I am confused!

MAN
Did you learn that in Acting Two?

INGE'NUE
I think you're being sarcastic.

MAN
Very perceptive.

AMANDA
And where do all these emotions come from?

WOMAN
From the actors.

AMANDA
From the playwright. You wouldn't exist without me.

WOMAN
Such chutzpah! Oh, you are making my head ache!

MAN
And mine! Do you call this snide play on words a play?

AMANDA
It is a play.

MAN
You can't have a play without conflict. That's a rule!

WOMAN
Yes, and you can't have a play without a climax! That's a rule!

MAN
And you can't have a play without a goal. What is my goal? Why am I
in this play?

AMANDA

So the audience will forget you starred in *The Turkey*.

INGE'NUE

(Pouting)

I don't want to play the inge'nue with a name like "Gidget"! I want to play an older woman like this older woman.

(Pointing to the WOMAN)

WOMAN

What do you mean an "older" woman? Are you trying to be insulting?

MAN

I insist on playing the villain!

(Goes into a hissy fit. To Amanda.)

You can't play the villain! I always play the villain! What will my fans say?

AMANDA

They'll remember you in *The Turkey*.

MAN

Now you are being insulting! I'm going to play the villain, or else! You're trying to take all the best parts! That isn't fair! You're only a playwright. Where would you be without us actors?

WOMAN

I want to play the villain for a change.

MAN

No, you can't do that! Do you think this is film noir?

INGE'NUE

What's film noir?

WOMAN

Oh, please! This is too much!

MAN
(To Amanda)
What kind of a playwright are you? This isn't a play! Where is the conflict? Where is the climax? Where is the denouement?

INGE'NUE
What's a. . . ?

MAN
Oh, shut up!

AMANDA
(Gesturing to the others as if teaching children.)
This is the play. This is the conflict, this is the climax, and this is the denouement.

MAN
This is the conflict?

WOMAN
And this is the climax?

INGE'NUE
What's a denouement?

MAN and WOMAN TOGETHER
Oh, shut up!

AMANDA
Shall we begin?

MAN
But this is a ten-minute play. Isn't this the end?

AMANDA

Yes, but the end is always a new beginning.
    (SHE encourages the audience to clap and calls out.)
Author! Author! Author!
        (SHE turns her back on the audience and takes a bow.
        SHE holds out her hands and the OTHERS join her.
        ALL hold hands and all bow with their backs to the
        audience. THEY wiggle their tails at the audience.)

THE END

SOUND OF THE RAIN

A Ten-Minute Romantic Drama

by

Jan Henson Dow

PRODUCTION NOTES

CAST OF CHARACTERS

Note: The role of Jennifer is played by two different actors representing two different ages in the life of the main character.

Jennifer — 39 years old, slim, dark hair

Jenny — 20s, slim, dark hair

Jordan — 40s, tall, someone who would be noticed in a crowd

SET
The empty set represents both The Players Club in New York City and a living room.

TIME
The present.

In memory of Robert Schroeder.

SOUND OF THE RAIN

(Although the stage is empty, it represents a reception at The Players Club in New York City.)

(SOFT SPOT UP on JENNIFER as she enters Stage Right. SHE is carrying an opened umbrella.)

JENNIFER

The night that I went to the reception at The Players Club it was raining. I almost decided not to go. It seemed so strange to go without Mark, without a husband. Strange after all these years together. "Don't be a fool," I thought. "You've got to start going out sometime. No one will lead you by the hand."

> (SHE closes the umbrella and puts it down. SPOT UP on JORDAN standing Down Left, a drink in his hand. SHE turns toward DL where JORDAN is standing.)

The room was crowded with people. Strange faces in a crowded room, but it was as if I were looking for someone. "I don't really know anyone," I thought. "But why do I feel I'm looking for someone?"

I looked across the room, and he was standing there against the wall, a drink in his hand, a little space all around him. I knew I had to go and meet him. "He's probably married and has six children," I thought. I hesitated, but I knew I had to walk across the room and meet him.

> (SHE crosses to Down Left.)

"Hello," I said. He looked at me. No, that's not the right word. He knew me. Oh, I don't mean that we had met before. I mean that he knew me and I knew him. As if we had always known each other.
       (To Jordan)
Forgive me. I know we haven't met. . . .

JORDAN

No, you're wrong. We have met.

JENNIFER

But we don't know each other.

JORDAN

Yes, we do know each other. I just don't know your name.

JENNIFER

Jennifer.

JORDAN

Jennifer — yes — Jordan. Let me get you a drink. What would you like?

JENNIFER

I don't know. Perhaps. . . .

JORDAN

A dry vermouth on the rocks. Stay right there. Don't move. Promise.

JENNIFER

I promise.

JORDAN

I don't want to lose you.
       (HE crosses to far Left and exits.)

JENNIFER

I watched him make his way through the crowd. He stood at the bar, taller than anyone else and, even in that crowd, keeping a little space around him. I waited for him as if I would always wait for him to come back, whatever happened.

(SPOT FADES on JENNIFER.)

JENNY
(SHE enters Down Right and stands in a SPOT as if speaking to her young husband, MARK.)
Mark, what is it? What's wrong? Tell me what you're thinking.

(SPOT UP on JENNIFER. Up Center and on JORDAN who enters Down Left.)

JENNIFER
Oh, Jordan, how could everything go so wrong? I thought no one could ever know me as you did.

JORDAN
I do know you, every part of you, every curve of you, and you know me.

JENNIFER
No, I don't know you! You lied to me!

JENNY
(As if speaking to MARK.)
Mark, you lied to me!

JORDAN
(To JENNIFER)
What do you mean?

JENNIFER
You aren't divorced! You were never divorced! You lied to me.

JORDAN
(To JENNIFER)
Jenny, I've never loved anyone as I love you. I've never been as close to anyone.

JENNIFER
What about your wife? Did you say that when you were fucking her?

JORDAN
She and I haven't slept in the same bed in years.

JENNY
(As if speaking to MARK.)
Another lie!

JENNIFER
To go with all your other lies!

JORDAN
(HE takes her by the shoulders.)
You love me! Say it!

JENNIFER and JENNY
Oh, leave me alone!

JORDAN
Say it! Say it!

JENNIFER
I do love you. I love you with all my heart. I can't stop loving you even when I know you lied to me.

JENNY
(As if speaking to MARK)
I feel lost.

JORDAN
(To JENNIFER)
Listen to me! I didn't plan that you'd walk into The Players Club that night. I didn't plan that we'd fall in love. It just happened. You can't control life.

JENNIFER
Control! My world is falling apart! Everything I believed about you is a lie!

JENNY
(As if speaking to MARK)
Don't lie to me anymore, Mark. Where were you?

JENNIFER
When we met, you said you were divorced. I believed you!

JORDAN
It isn't as simple as you think.

JENNY
(As if speaking to MARK)
Mark, you were with someone else, weren't you?

JENNIFER
Why did you lie to me?

JORDAN
You know why. If I told you the truth that night when we met, that I was married, would you have stayed with me?

JENNIFER
I don't know. But you didn't give me a choice!

JORDAN
That's your answer. I couldn't take the chance of losing you.

JENNIFER and JENNY

I trusted you!

JENNY
(As if speaking to MARK)
Not to leave me when I needed you!

JENNIFER

Not to lie to me when I needed you! When you were away those long months, without caring how I felt, did you think I would just sit on a shelf waiting for you to come back?

JENNY
(As if speaking to MARK)
Just tell me the truth!

JENNIFER

Just tell me the truth!

JORDAN

Do you really want the truth? You don't need me. You want me and I want you, but you don't need me. My wife has been ill for a long time. She panics when she has to go out. She can function as long as she knows I'll come back. We have two sons. You know that. I couldn't leave them when they needed me. I can't leave them now. That's the truth.

JENNIFER

I see. Now I'm going to tell you the truth. See if you can stand it.

JENNIFER and JENNY
(JENNIFER speaking to JORDAN and JENNY to MARK)

No more lies between us anymore.

JENNIFER

When you were away those long months, I had an affair with someone else.

JORDAN

(Stunned)

You – you were with someone else?

(HE grabs her by the shoulders.)

You were in his arms! You let him touch you — the way I touch you!

JENNIFER

No one can touch me the way you touch me.

JORDAN

Liar!

JENNY

(As if speaking to MARK)

I promised to be faithful! I kept my promise!

JORDAN

Faithful?

JENNIFER

What promise have you kept?

JORDAN

My God, Jenny! Why did you do it?

JENNIFER

Why did I do it? Do you think there's a simple answer? It was something I had to do, to break your spell over me.

JENNY

(As if speaking to MARK)

I was at home with my parents.

JENNIFER

And then I was married to Mark. And then I met you. I thought we were meant to be together. Then I found out you lied to me.

JORDAN

And you've lied to me!

JENNIFER

Yes. I didn't know who I was anymore.

JENNY
(As if speaking to MARK)
Where is the woman I thought I would be?

JENNIFER

Don't you see? If I only live in the mirror of men's eyes . . .

JENNY

. . . as if gazing into a dark pool.

JENNIFER

I could do that – go down into that dark pool. But I would have to give up something in myself I value — some quiet place. I had to choose. Just as you had to choose.

JORDAN

Jenny, don't leave me! I need you!

JENNIFER

No, she needs you. You said it yourself.

JORDAN

Jenny. . . !

JENNIFER

It's all right. I understand more than you know. I'll never love anyone

as I love you. I'll never want anyone as I want you. I only know that
I've got to get away from you for now. To put some distance between
us . . .

JENNY
(As if speaking to MARK)
. . . to find out who I am.
(JENNY exits Down Right.)

JORDAN
Jenny. . . !

JENNIFER
Don't follow me. Just — let me go.

JORDAN
Jenny! Jenny!

(SPOT FADES on JORDAN)

JENNIFER
(SHE picks up the umbrella. SHE is alone in SOFT
SPOT at Center.)
Do you remember the night we walked by the park.
It had been raining, and the streetlights were glowing
In the mist, and as we walked we made the world anew,
like gods, from rain and mist and night and joy,
"Promise that you'll never forget this moment.
Listen, it is the happiest moment of my life.
Whatever comes. I have loved and been loved,
and that can never change. Promise you'll remember
when I loved you with all my heart."
It was night. We were walking by the park,
and the streetlights were glowing in the rain.

(JENNIFER opens the umbrella and slowly exits.

SLOW FADE to BLACK leaving only SOFT
LIGHTS GLOWING in the mist.)

THE END

TEN-MINUTE MONOLOGUES

DANCIN' AT THE APPLE JACK

A Ten-Minute Monologue

by

Jan Henson Dow

PRODUCTION NOTES

CAST OF CHARACTERS

Eula Mae Rogers — 65, short, slightly plump

SET
The stage is bare except for a wooden bench.

For Julie Dow, my wonderful daughter-in-law.

DANCIN' AT THE APPLE JACK

(EULA MAE ROGERS enters Stage Right. Crosses. SHE starts to pass the bench, almost crossing to Stage Left, SHE glances back, turns, and crosses to the bench and then pauses.)

EULA MAE
(As if speaking to someone who is sitting on the bench.)
Why, hello, Honey. You don't mind if I share this bench with you?

(Pause)

Why, thank you, I appreciate it.

(SHE sits on the bench)

I saw you when I was walkin' by this morning and I saw you was still sittin' here on my way back. I just thought, I'll sit down and rest a spell. Pass the time of day. My, it's hot.

(Pause)

It's usual this time of year. But it's cool under these shade trees. It's one of my favorite spots. Just sittin' here, watchin' the creek flow by.

(SHE holds out her hand as if offering to shake hands.)

My name is Eula Mae Rogers; what's yours?

(Pause.)

Why that's a real pretty name. Real pretty. You look just like your name. Now you take "Eula Mae". That's kind of an old fashioned name. I was named after my great aunt, Eula Mae Gibbins, who was raised and buried over at Settler's Hollow. Oh, you don't know where that's at? It's the next hop over to Johnsonville. Well, that's just up the road from – well, it don't matter none.

(Pause.)

You waitin' for the bus?

(Pause.)

It'll probably be late. It usually is.

(Pause.)

There's only the one and they've been talkin' about closing that down.

(Pause.)

Where you from, Honey?

(Pause.)

All over? Well, you must have done a lot of travelin'. Are you on your way to Pittsburgh?

(Pause.)

Well, it's nothin' to me, but Pittsburgh is where this bus is goin', in case you're interested.

(Pause.)

You know, I've traveled a fair piece myself. Up to Detroit and Chicago and even down to Florida once. I never could see why folks move away from their kin to a place like Florida.

(Pause.)

I wouldn't want to live down there though, too hot and full of bugs and hurricanes.

(Pause.)

If you don't mind my askin', how old are you, Honey?

(Pause.)

That's young to be travelin' around by yourself. Don't your people worry about you.

(Pause.)

Oh, I see. That's hard not havin' any people to go home to.

(Pause.)

Oh, I'm sorry. I didn't mean to pry.

(SHE stands up as if to follow after her new friend.)

Don't go off mad. Come on now and sit back down. That backpack looks kind of heavy. I'll just keep my big mouth shut.

(SHE sits on the bench.)

Guess I've just got too talkative, but I don't mean nothin' by it. That's what happens when you get older. You think because you've lived all these years, you can tell other people how to do it. But that never works out. Everbody's got to figure things out for himself.

(Pause.)

Me? I'll be sixty-five this comin' January.

(Pause.)

Well, thank you, Honey. I don't feel that old either. "You're as young as you feel", I always say.

(Pause.)

My, that is a nice breeze. I just love to sit here and listen to that creek flowin' by.

(Pause.)

It's called Stony Lonesome cause it's full of stones and it does seem kind of lonesome just flowin' along by itself. But it's real pretty, sparklin' in the sun.

(Pause.)

When I was young, I used to like to skip a stone across the water clear to the other side. See if I could get it all the way across.

(SHE gets up and picks up a stone and throws it.)

Oh, my, guess I've lost my pitchin' arm. You want to try?

(As if giving HER new friend a stone.)

Like this.

(Pause.)

Well, we both need a little practice.

(Pause.)

Yes, just up the road.

(SHE points up the road.)

See that hill. I live just around the next bend. The yellow house with the green shutters. The one that needs paintin'.

(Pause.)

I've got folks all up and down these hollers. I was born right here and lived here it seems forever. But sometimes it seems only yesterday. I can still see me on the way to school that first day, holdin' my mother's hand. And when she left, I held up a book in front of my face so the others wouldn't see me cryin'. Seems just like yesterday.

(Pause.)

Once in a while I think life is like a dream or like this creek just flowin' along.

(Pause. SHE crosses and sits on the bench.)

Are you married, Honey?

(Pause.)

I didn't think so. You not wearin' a ring and all.

(Pause.)

This little ole ring? It's not much, but that's all Cal could afford. Times were hard in those days. Still are up here in these mountains with the coal about played out.

(Pause.)

No, I'm a widow now. Cal's been dead five goin' on six years. But I still wear this ring. Reminds me of our good times together.

(Pause.)

Well, they weren't all good times. They never are. You gotta take the bitter with the sweet. In his younger days Cal was hard livin' and hard drinkin', and when he wasn't drinkin', he was kind of boring, if you know what I mean. All into himself, like so many men. I don't know why they're like that. Guess they don't want to let on they have feelings.

(Pause.)

If you ask me, I think Cal never did get over his daddy dyin' in that mine explosion.

(Pause.)

You never heard of that explosion? It was in all the papers. Eighteen killed and Cal's daddy was one of them. Cal said when his daddy went down in that hole, he never knowd if he'd ever come out. And he never did.

(Pause.)

Cal blamed it all on the owners. What with black lung, cave-ins, gas explosions, Cal said the owners didn't give a damn what happened to the miners as long as the fat cats got theirs. Cal said he'd be damned if he'd ever go down in the mines like his daddy, and he never did.

When he'd get one of his blue spells, I'd ask him, "What's the matter? You seem kind of down in the dumps.

And he'd say, "Well, you ought to know."

And I'd say, "Well, if you tell me, then I'd know."

And he'd say, "If you think you know so much, you tell me."

He always tried to get in the last word. . . .

(Pause.)

Men! You can't live with them and you can't live without 'em.

(Laughing.)

Ain't that the truth!

(Pause.)

Me? Oh, I've done all kinds of things. Waited tables over at the Betty Luncheonette. Nurse's aide at the retirement home and over at the hospital in Pritchardville. I've just turned my hand at whatever come along. You lookin' for a job?

(Getting up from the bench as if following her new friend.)

I'm sorry. Now don't take offense. I don't think you look like "some kind of bum." I just thought you travelin' around, you might need a job.

(Pause.)

I know you're not lookin' for any kind of handout. I just thought about

Betty, over at the Luncheonette. I could put in a good word for you. It don't pay much, but it's a start.

(Pause.)

Well, it was just a thought.

(Pause.)

I could see why you wouldn't want to stay around here.

(Pause.)

Well, I wouldn't call it "crappy" exactly.

(Pause.)

Guess it must seem half asleep to someone just travelin' through. But you wouldn't believe all the squabblin' and carryin' on around here.

(Pause.)

What about? Well, if I'm going to tell you the whole story, I'd have to go back to just after Cal died.

(Pause.)

Cancer. Smoked two packs not countin' the beer. I told him, "Cal, you should try and quit." But he wouldn't listen. He was the stubbornest man I ever knew. But after he died, I kind of missed not havin' anybody to fight with or cook for. If the truth be told, I was real blue.

(Pause.)

My kids? All three moved up North, Earle and Howard to Chicago. Janelle and the kids are in Detroit. Her husband worked in an auto plant. All the kids had to go North to find work, but with the plants closing and all, they may have to come back home and start over. Of course, they all came back for Cal's funeral.

(Pause.)

You haven't lived, Honey, 'til you've been to a small town Southern funeral. People bringin' pies and cakes and casseroles, you wouldn't believe. Sittin' on the porch, tellin' you they knew your grandpappy. We didn't have to do a lick of cookin' for a whole week. Cal was sure well liked around these parts.

(Pause.)

But after the kids all left, I got real blue, not havin' Cal to kick around anymore. But then one day, sittin' on the porch, rockin' and waitin' to grow old, bored as Hell, if you pardon my French, I had a revelation, kind of like. Like a light just come down and zapped me. Like I was born again.

(Pause.)

Oh, my no, Honey, I wasn't saved or anything like that.

(Pause.)

Are you saved, Honey?

(Pause.)

I'm glad to hear it. When my friend, Wilma Jean, asks me if I'm saved, I say, "Saved? From what?"

(Pause.)

No, it was like a light come down and zapped me, and I said to myself,

"Eula Mae", I said. "You are not getting any younger and that's the truth. Whatever you want to do, you better get up and do it now instead of sittin' here, waitin' to die."

(Pause.)

It was Cal dyin' that made me see the light. Him dyin' with all his dreams unfulfilled. You see, Cal worked since high school, down at the A-1 Body Shop. He was one of the best around, but he always wanted to go on down to Daytona and be a race car driver. He never did though, not even for a visit. He kept sayin' he had too many mouths to feed.

(Pause.)

But that wasn't it. He was afraid to try new things, afraid of what he might find out.

I kept sayin', "Cal, you ought to go on down there and look it over." But he never did.

(Pause.)

I remembered that, after he died and I said to myself, "Eula Mae, you better get up and start livin' and try new things cause this is all you've got."

(Pause.)

What kind of new things? I always wanted to try dancin'. So right then and there I decided I wanted to learn to dance. You see, my folks never did allow us to dance when I was young, thinkin' it was sinful and all. So I said to myself, "Eula Mae, you need a little sin 'cause you ain't had much, and you never know 'til you try."

(Pause.)

So one Saturday night, I went on over to The Apple Jack and just started in' and I've been dancin' ever since. Line dancin', zydeco – boogie is my favorite. You should see me "get on down" and boogie!

(Pause.)

The Apple Jack? Why that's a roadhouse over on the edge of town. Raf Peachum just showed up one day, said he saw a real need in this town, a place to go and have a good time. So he got a judge to throw out an old ordnance against dancin' that's been on the books since Calvin Coolidge. He hired Foxy Wilson to jockey the music, and every Saturday night he started havin' dancin'. And that stirred up a hornet's nest, I can tell you.

(Pause.)

That loud mouth Eldred Slocum started preachin' to the holy rollers, gettin' everyone all fired up about dancin' being the next best thing to fornication, enticing young people into sin.

Finally they got the City Council riled up, and they recollected an old ordinance on the books that denied dance permits to anyone who was not a person of "good moral character". Tried to get the police chief to issue a summons. He said he was plannin' to as soon as he consulted the mayor. But when the Council started talkin' about a Constitutional Amendment against dancin', then the fat was in the fire!

And I said to myself, who are they to claim they're the only ones "of good moral character?" Who are they to start changing the Constitution? And I said to myself, "Eula Mae, would you rather be dancin' on Saturday night and havin' a good time or pullin' a long face with that holier-than-thou crowd who wouldn't know a good time if it walked up and bit them in the ass?" Well, it weren't no contest.

When Raf said he'd be damned if he'd be run off, he took the whole city council to court and got the ordnance struck down. Then he threw the biggest party this town has ever seen. We all just turned out at the Apple and started to boogie. And I've been dancin' ever since. Every Saturday night, I just put on my jeans and checked shirt and leather vest and just go on over. Dancin' at The Apple Jack just sort of liberated my heart and soul.

You should see all the young people who turn out on Saturday night. When Foxie Wilson starts the music, we all just head to the dance floor and start to boogie. I just grab whoever's standin' by or dance by myself. It don't make no never mind to me. It's all just dancin' and havin' a good time and letting everybody do his own thing.

Do you dance, Honey?

(Pause.)

I don't know that one. You'll have to teach me that one.

(Pause.)

Oh, that's right, I forgot. You're waitin' for the next bus out.

(Pause.)

You know what, I just thought of something. There's always another bus tomorrow. If you don't have any place special you're goin', you could come on home with me. You look like you could use a good home cooked meal. Why, you could stay the night.

(Pause.)

Honey, it's no trouble. I've got all those spare bedrooms with the kids up North and all. You know, Honey, you look kind of all tired out and a little peaked. Like you could use a little rest.

(As if patting HER new friend's hand.)

Now that's all right. You can cry if you want to. I've done plenty of that in my time. I've got a tissue here somewhere.

(SHE looks in her pocket as if pulling out a tissue and offering it to her friend.)

It's a little used, but don't mind that.

(Pause.)

There now. You could stay a while with me. I've got plenty of room. I could even get you a job over at the Betty.

(Pause.)

Why, you're not puttin' me out any. I'd like the company.

(Stands up.)

You and me, we'll get to know each other. On Saturday night, I'll take you on over to The Apple and introduce you to all the young people.

(Pause.)

Oh, that's right. I know you're only planin' to stay the one night. But if you change your mind, and stay 'til Sunday you and me could go on over to The Apple. I'll introduce you to all the young people over there. They all know me. They say, "Come on, Gran Ma, let's boogie," and we do. 'Cause, Honey, if I've learned one thing, it's this: You only go around once, so whatever comes along, you got to jump right in and start to boogie.

(SHE gets up from the bench.)

You need any help with that backpack?

(Pause.)

I know you can carry it. But we all need a little help some times. When we get home, we'll rest a little and then you can help me fix supper.

(SHE exits still talking to her new friend.)

THE END

PUTTY SING IS MISSING

A Ten-Minute Comic Monologue

by

Jan Henson Dow

PRODUCTION NOTES

CAST OF CHARACTERS

Clarise — a middle aged woman, slightly overweight but expensively dressed in slacks and a top with numerous necklaces and bracelets and a large ring

SET

A living room in an upscale, adult gated community somewhere in the South. Three chairs at Stage Center Right represent a sofa.

PROPS

A magazine on the sofa.
A phone on the sofa.

For Diane and Harry DiSalvio.

PUTTY SING IS MISSING

CLARISE
(Enters from Up Stage Left, calling.)
Putty Sing! Putty Sing!

(Exits Down Stage Left. Enters again at Left.)

Putty Sing! Where are you? Mumsie is trying to find you!

(No luck, exasperated.)
Oh, Drat!

(Picks up phone which is on the sofa. Dials. Talking on the phone, SHE is distraught.)

Oh, Shirley! Shirley! Is that you?

(Listening.)

Who else would be speaking in your voice? I don't think that's funny. That's not funny at all! Not at a time like this!

(Beginning to sob, pacing to Stage Right and back to Center.)

Oh, Shirley! I am beside myself!

(Listening.)

What else is new? Oh, Shirley, something terrible has happened! I am simply out of my mind with worry!

(Listening.)

I said, "with worry!" Not just "out of my mind!"

(Listening.)

Well what is it now? Oh, Shirley! Putty Sing is missing!

(Listening, Stands.)

I said, "missing," not "pissing!" Shirley, Putty Sing's been kidnapped!

(Listening.)

Who in their right mind would want to kidnap Putty Sing? Anybody, that's who. She's a very valuable dog! You know she costs $2,000 with shots and a haircut and those adorable little outdoor booties!

(Listening.)

What do you mean they'll bring her back when she starts pooping all over the house! That is a mean thing to say! Shirley, you used to be my best friend. You've got to come on over here and help me find her! I've been looking for her up, down, and sideways!

(Pacing, Listening.)

What? Why don't I call her baby sitter? Well, that is a tragic story.

(Sits on the sofa, Listening.)

You have an appointment with your hair dresser in ten minutes? Well this won't take long. You remember that new baby sitter I was trying out? Well, when I went out to dinner with my Mah-Jongg Club, the baby sitter drove Putty Sing to Hardeeville without my permission.

(Listening.)

To Hardeeville. To visit her brother.

(Listening.)

Yes, the one who had his front teeth knocked out with a chain saw. That's the one. And she had a flat tire on the way. There they were on I-95 with cars just whizzin' by.

(Listening.)

What?
                (Gets up and paces, Listening.)

She doesn't have Triple A. That's why she's a baby sitter. Her brother had to buy a new tire at Walmart and change it right there on the side of the road.

(Stands.)

When I found out she drove Putty Sing across county lines, I could have spit nails. She didn't bring her back until after midnight, and I had to fix her two sandwiches so she had the strength to drive on home. I'm getting another baby sitter if it's the last thing I do!

(Pause.)

Shirley, are you still there?

(Listening.)

Why don't I call Darlene, my new best friend? Well if you want to know, she and I had a falling out over Mah-Jongg.

(Listening.)

No, I was not caught stealing her favorite tiles. Darlene's never been reliable when it comes to games of chance. Not like you, Shirley. You've got to come on over here right away and help me find Putty Sing!

(Listening.)

Stick the tiles up my. . . !

(SHE is visibly shocked.)

That's a very rude thing to say!

(SHE hangs up and tosses the phone on the sofa. SHE exits Right and enters again.)

Putty Sing, where are you? Oh, Baby, I don't mind a bit you chewing up your darlin' little booties. Oh, I don't know what to do!

(SHE sits and picks up a copy of the community magazine which is lying on the sofa. SHE looks up a number in the magazine. SHE picks up the phone, calls.)

Is this the Main Gate?

(Listening.)

What is my CAM number? I don't remember my CAM number.

(Listening.)

Well, it's somewhere on the card in the bottom of my purse which is on the table in the bedroom.

(Listening.)

I know I need a CAM number to leave a pass at the gate. Do you think I'm an idiot?

(Listening.)

Did you say "pass" or what I think you said?

(Listening.)

No, I don't want to leave a pass. I need you to send someone over here right away!

(Listening.)

What's the problem?

(Stands.)

Putty Sing has been kidnapped!

(Listening.)

Don't be so literal. She's not a kid! She's a dog, a cute little miniature poodle and she weights only three pounds and she's peach colored.

(Listening.)

If I call 911 and report a dognapping they'll think I'm demented.

(Listening.)

We do not pay you $7.25 an hour to make smart remarks!

> (Slams down the phone. Looks up another number in the magazine. Calls the number.)

Is this the main office?

> (Listening.)

Now listen carefully. I have a serious problem over here and I need help right away!

> (Listening.)

No, I have not fallen out of my wheel chair! My adorable little Putty Sing has been dognapped!

> (Listening.)

CLARISE

Putty Sing!

> (Listening.)

What kind of a name is that? It's a cute way of saying, "Pretty Thing" with a lisp.

> (SHE lisps.)

"Putty Sing." Got it?

> (Listening.)

No, this is not some kind of joke! Hello! Hello!

> (Slams down the phone. Distraught.)

Oh, what am I going to do?

(Picks up the phone and calls.)

Fred, is that you?

(Listening.)

No, I have not gone gaga! Of course I know the voice of my own brother. What are you doing right now?

(Listening.)

Watching TV? Well, you're going to have to get out of that Lazy Boy and come on over here. Putty Sing is missing!

(Listening.)

No, I did not leave her in the garage! What kind of a person do you take me for?

(Listening. Stands.)

Fred, once and for all, I did not steal that Statue of Liberty you bought in New York City! Fred, you were ten years old! You lost it! Got it? You lost it!

(Listening.)

No, I did not steal it! You've got to let it go! Get a life, Fred! Get a life!

(Listening.)

Watching NCIS on TV is not "a life"! You've got to come on over here and help me find Putty Sing!

(Listening.)

You can't? Louise has the car? Where's she gone now?

(Listening.)

That woman is a shopaholic! Well, when she comes back next Christmas, call me.

(SHE hangs up the phone and sits and thinks for a minute.)

Well, desperate times require desperate measures.

(She stands and calls a number.)

Walter, is that you?

(Listening.)

I've already heard that one, and it wasn't funny the first time.

(Listening.)

What in the hell am I calling you for? Oh, Walter, Putty Sing has been kidnapped!

(Listening.)

Putty Sing – my new puppy.

(Listening.)

Maybe she was eaten by an alligator? Well, that's not a nice thing to say! Walter, I need help and all I get is one of your smart remarks.

(Listening.)

What do I expect you to do about it? I'd like you to remember we were married for twenty-nine years come next Wednesday.

(Listening.)

How could you forget the sinking of the Titanic? Walter, we'll discuss that disaster another time. I need your help!

(Listening.)

That's a fine attitude. If I knew where else to turn, would I call you? I need your help!

(Listening.)

Why not ask Frank? Walter, Frank's been dead for four years!

(Listening.)

From the neck up? Walter, that was always your problem. You had no heart.
(Beat.)

And not much else either.

(Listening.)

No, I do not want to start a fight.

(SHE, of course, does want to start a fight.)

If I wanted to start a fight, I'd start by saying, "How's that cheap trick you married after you dumped me?"

(Pause.)

Walter? Walter? Are you still there?

(SHE looks at the phone. HE has obviously hung up.)

That was your problem all along. You lacked the art of conversation.

(Exasperated, she puts down the phone.)

Oh, what do I do now?

(SHE sits and picks up the magazine and thumbs through it. She speaks as if she is saying a four letter word.)

F. F. F. F. Oh here it is. "Fix It".

(SHE calls a number.)

Is this Mr. Fix It?

(Listening.)

Do you remember me, when I called you last spring after I lost my diamond ring?

(Listening.)

That's right. I'm the one who cancelled after I found it hidden in a sock under my mattress.

(Listening.)

What's the crisis now?

(Stands.)

I am desperate! That's what!

(Listening.)

No, my toilet is not overflowing. It's my little dog. She's gone missing.

(Listening.)

I've already heard that one today. How much do you charge by the hour to come on over here?

(Listening.)

$60 just to walk in the door! Well,

(Beat.)

How much do you charge if you just stand on the porch?

(Listening.)

Oh, all right. When can you come?

(Listening.)

A month from next Tuesday? She may be dead by then!

(Listening.)

Well if I can't find someone else more reliable, I'll have to call you back. Goodbye.

(SHE hangs up.)

Oh, men are so heartless. Who can I call now? Maybe I'll call my dentist. He's into pain.

(Beat.)

No, I'd just get that receptionist who thinks her boobs are the best thing since sliced bread.

(Walks around, very upset.)

Oh, I just don't know what I'm going to do if I don't find her!

(Dejected, SHE sits on the sofa. SHE makes the sound of a small puppy.)

Um – Um – Um – Um.

(Leans over and looks under the sofa.)

Putty Sing, is that you?

(Gets down on hands and knees to look under the sofa.)

Putty Sing, are you under there?

(SHE sees Putty Sing lying under the sofa and responds with joy.)

Putty! Putty! How in the world did you get stuck under the sofa?

(Wags her tail toward the audience as if she is a puppy dog.)

Putty! Come here, Baby. Putty! Come on here now! That's it! You can do it! Just come on out! You can do it!

(SHE reaches under the sofa and pulls Putty Sing out. [Note: Putty Sing is a real dog, but the audience must imagine CLARISE is holding her.] Scolding, but with great fondness, SHE holds Putty Sing up.)

Oh, you bad girl! You're just a bad girl!

(SHE kisses Putty Sing on the nose and then holds Putty Sing close in her arms and hugs her.)

Oh, that's all right. Mumsie isn't mad at you.

(Petting Putty Sing.)

Do you know what we're going to do? We're going to go right out this very minute and buy you a new toy and a new pair of booties. That's exactly what we're going to do. We're going to buy you a pair of red booties and a new toy that squeaks. I'm just so glad you're home! What would I do without you, Baby? What would I do without you?

(Holding Putty Sing close, CLARISE rapidly exits at Left.)

THE END

MIKE'S ANGST

A Ten-Minute Monologue

by

Jan Henson Dow

PRODUCTION NOTES

CAST OF CHARACTERS

Mike Reynolds — 44, not "pretty boy" handsome, but good looking, with something of an attitude, which is attractive to women.

SET
A bare stage which represents a living room, with a single, comfortable chair.

TIME
The present.

In memory of Scott Dow.

MIKE'S ANGST

MIKE

Now I know you're not going to believe this story! You are not going to believe it, but I swear, it's all true. Well, most of it's true. I mean, who could tell the whole story — like trying to grab a cloud. How do you get a handle on it. So, this is the condensed version, okay?

It goes like this. One Sunday I'm sitting around watching the game on TV.

(Sitting in the chair as if watching a game, HE is excited.)

Go! Go! Go! Are you blind! That was a hole you could have driven a truck through, you bum! Jeez! You couldn't hold your ball if it was attached to your leg! You overpaid felon!

(HE clicks off the TV.)

That's it! That's it! I've had it with football! They just give them the bank and let them stumble around with it! I've had it with football! And with baseball! And just about every other damned thing!! I've had it! Up to here!

Look, I'm this guy in my 40's, well 44 to be exact. Got this good job, my condo all paid for, SUV paid for. I've got no problems, no problems at all. So — what's the problem? Well, I'm watching this game when I start thinking about Mel Gibson. No it's not what you think, although

it's all right if you want to think that. I don't have any problem with that.
You know the old joke, "Some of my best friends are. . . ." Whatever.
But it's not that. There's a different reason I'm thinking about Mel
Gibson.

I'm feeling this — well, "angst" is the word. It's not a good word. I
don't like that word "angst," but that's what I'm feeling. No, it's not
what you think. It's not women — well, it's always women, but this
time, it's not "women" exactly.

It's like this. My last relationship had just broken up. Finished, kaput.
One of a long line of "relationships" stretching back to — infinity.
They come and they go. Take this last "relationship." Well, I couldn't
even call it a "relationship." She was flying into the city and I was flying
back and I had to stop over in the city on business. I was on one of
those, God, you know, one of those flights that flies into LaGuardia.
No — no, tries to fly into LaGuardia. Never go there! If you want to
get a life, never never go to LaGuardia! It's the pits!

So we were waiting at O'Hare, sitting on the tarmac for three hours,
for God's sake, for a parking space at LaGuardia! It was either storm
the cockpit or start talking to this good looking blonde in the next seat.
Well, one thing leads to another and there we are six months later. She
wouldn't leave her high powered job in Chicago if I wouldn't commit,
and I didn't feel, you know, ready and I wouldn't leave my job and so it
goes. "Relationships!" I've had it with "relationships!"

As I was saying, I was sitting here , watching the game, thinking about
Mel Gibson. Now women have said I'm not bad looking — not Mel
Gibson good-looking, but who is? Probably not even Mel Gibson. Now,
I don't envy his looks, don't get me wrong. It's not his looks. It's something
else. It's, well, he's married and has seven, maybe eight, kids. They just
keep popping up like toast. Stick it in and up pops another one.

And me — I'm sitting here, trying to watch the game, but all the time
I'm thinking, I don't have any children — a long string of "relationships"
— live in, live out, weekend, one night — but I always — move on.

But that's not the story I want to tell. It's like this. I'm sitting here thinking about Mel Gibson and his eight kids, or whatever, when the phone rings and I answer it.

(HE answers HIS phone.)

A woman's voice on the other end of the line says, "Is this Michael Reynolds?"

And I say, "Don't try to sell me anything. I've got everything I could possibly want. I'm not interested! Just take me off your list."

And she says, "No, wait. I don't want to sell you anything. I called because — well, are you Mike Reynolds?"

"Who is this?" I say, getting suspicious.

"Were you at Missouri State University?" And when she said that a cold chill went through me. I knew — I knew what she was going to say next.

I felt like I was looking down the barrel of a gun. "Yeah, I was at Missouri State." And what she said next blew me away.

"Do you remember Lori?" she said.

Do I remember Lori? My heart, sort of — turned over and my stomach with it.

(HE turns to Stage Right.)

And I'm twenty years old again, seeing this blonde walk by eating an apple. She was wearing a blue sweater, one that matched her eyes, and she was carrying a psychology text. I turn on a dime and follow her to class and sit next to her.

(HE sits.)

I sort of lean over and whisper, "What's the assignment?"

She sort of gives me a look. "I never saw you here before," she says.

"That's because I've never been here before. I just followed you in."

And she laughs. She always had the funniest laugh. She could crack me up with laughing. So I guess that tells you everything you need to know about how we met.

(HE stands and crosses to Stage Left.)

My father had gone out to Missouri State with his new wife, and my mom, she was always trying to get us connected, thought I should go out to Missouri, try to make contact. Fat chance. His new wife didn't want to know me. I don't blame her. That's not true. I do blame her. But she didn't last long , which is fine with me, but that's another story.

So I enroll in the university where my father was teaching at the time. A year after I moved out there, my dad took another job in Alabama. What was I supposed to do — follow him around wondering if he even knew I was there? So much for my mom's usual attempt to engineer my life.

But about Lori. It was the last year of the war. I was serving my time doing what we all did, drinking beer, stoned, staging protests, playing guitar, chasing co-eds, and flunking out. Wondering, should I go to Canada? Where in the hell was Canada, and how do you get there?

(HE picks up the phone.)

And then this phone call out of the blue and out of the past that I thought I had left behind. "Lori?" I said and my heart sort of turned over.

"No, I'm Lori's daughter. If you're Mike Reynolds and you were at

Missouri State, then I'm your daughter, too." And my stomach dropped another two feet.

I was stunned. I didn't know what to say. I just stood there with my jaw hanging open, not knowing what to say.

"Hello, are you there?" she said, a bit anxious as if I'd hang up on her.

Then I said the dumbest thing I could think of. "How did you find me?" As if I was 20 years old again and didn't know who I was and didn't want anyone to find me, least of all myself.

(HE puts down the phone and half lies on the chairs.)

I remember the last time I saw Lori. As if it was yesterday. It was a Saturday and she was walking into my bedroom, the one with those tie-dyed curtains and the broken down springs that squeaked when we made love. Man, did they squeak.

I remember it as if it was yesterday. I was lying back in bed, playing the guitar, the one Crystal stomped on when she shouted, "You asshole!" and stormed out. Well, let's face it. She was right. I was an asshole, but she didn't have to break my guitar. But that's another story.

As I said, Lori is walking into the room, and I say, "Hay, Babe. What's goin' down?" Expecting her to say, "You are," and jump on me. But she just stood there, with a funny look on her face, as if she didn't know who I was.

Then she took a deep breath and said, "I'm going to have a baby." And she just stood there waiting for me to say something.

And I didn't know what to say — stoned, playing guitar, flunking out, about to be drafted. . . . I couldn't fit her news into that life. Talk about angst. I invented that term even if I couldn't spell it.

We just looked at each other for a long time as if she was expecting me to say something. I didn't know what to say. I was stunned. I didn't even get up off the bed.

Then she turned away and her shoulders sort of sagged and when she turned back it was like she had walked through a door and closed it behind her.

"You don't have to worry," she said. "I've already told my parents. They said to come on home and they'd take care of the adoption and everything." She had already told them, and they had made other plans, and I wasn't even included.

Then she just walked out of the room and out of my life, and I didn't try to stop her.

(HE sits up.)

Oh, I tried to call, left messages. But she wouldn't call me back. And then, she was gone, and I heard she'd left school.

Seven months later there was a note. It wasn't even signed. "It's a girl." That's all she wrote, and that was the end of that, until the voice on the phone said my name.

(HE holds up the phone.)

"Are you Mike Reynolds?"

"Hello, are you still there?" she said.

And then it hit me. I had never been there, not for her, not for Lori. I had never been there for either of them.

Oh, I had wondered what happened to Lori, what happened to the baby, where she was, what she was like, but I knew that was all in the past. I never tried to find her. She wouldn't want to know me, so why bother?

What would she say anyhow? "You louse! You ran out on me!" No, I had never been there for her — never been there, never done that.

"Hello," she said. "Hello, are you there?"

"Yes, I'm here." I didn't say, "You've got the wrong guy. I'm not that Mike Reynolds. I don't know anyone named Lori." I said, "How did you find me?"

After she turned 21, she could find her birth records, find out the name of her birth parents. Her adoptive mom and dad were great. They said, "Go for it. If you don't, you'll always regret it."

"Always regret it," I thought — yeah, right.

'Lori wasn't hard to find."

(Thoughtfully.)

Lori had never been hard to find.

"Funny thing," she said, "Lori lives only two hours away. We've become really good friends — not like mother and daughter but really good friends. She told me your name, and I looked up Mike Reynolds on the Internet."

"You looked me up on the Internet?"

"Well, not you exactly. You wouldn't believe how many Mike Reynolds I called. I was going to call all of them."

"You were going to call all of them?"

"I would have," she said, "until I found the right one."

And when she said that, there was a warm glow that started down in the pit of my stomach. She was going to call all of them until she found the right one. Not just anyone, all of them, until she found the right one. And she knew, and I knew, that somehow she had found the right one.

"You wouldn't believe how nice the others were when I asked them. They said they were sorry and good luck and hoped I'd find the right one. I called so many, I thought I might have to give up."

And then she said something I know you're not going to believe. Because life is so crazy, but I swear it's true. She said Lori finally remembered the name of my buddy who shared the apartment, Stanislovski Waldenstein, good old Stan, the optometrist in Lindenwood, New Jersey. Stanislovski Waldenstein! Not many of those on the Internet. Stan said he knew the "Mike Reynolds" she was looking for and gave her my number, and that led her to me.

"Good old, Stan," I said. "He always keeps in touch."

"You haven't asked me my name," she said.

And I said another dumb thing, "Your name?" As if that's the first time I ever knew people had names. "Sure, what is your name?" As if I didn't much care one way or the other. I think I was afraid if she told me, I'd wake up and it would all be a dream.

And then she told me her name, and I swear to God, I knew her name would be Erin and it would be the most beautiful name in the world. "Erin," it's like music. It sings.

And then we talked for over an hour, and I found out she had graduated from the university and had a good job in St. Louis and had a boyfriend. They were thinking about getting married. Who would believe it? I have a daughter who graduated from college and is thinking about getting married!

Just before we hung up, I asked about Lori. She said Lori has two children who are just going into college. "I'll tell her I found you," she said.

"Do that. Tell her you found me. Tell her I said hello." Another dumb thing to say. "Tell her I said hello." Well, what could I say? "I never said goodbye, so tell her I said hello."

But I didn't say that. There are some things you can't put into words. I said, "Erin, I'm really glad you called. We'll keep in touch."

"Don't you want my address and phone number?"

"Sure, what is it?"

> (HE looks in HIS pocket for a pen and paper and writes down the number and address.)

And we hung up.

> (HE hangs up and sits down.)

I sat there for a long time, trying to absorb all this, trying to decide, "What do I do now?"

So the first thing I did was call my mom.

> (HE picks up the phone and makes a call.)

I didn't tell her my name. She already knows that. I started off with another dumb line, "Oh, by the way, there's something I never told you." Right! There's something I never told you." I always figured what she didn't know wouldn't hurt her, and believe me, there was plenty she didn't know.

But this time I knew what she would say. No, it's not what you think: Not, "Why did you do this and how could you do that?" My mom's pretty cool.

She said what I knew she would say, "Oh, Mike, thank God, you have a daughter! What's her name? Where does she live? What's her address?

What's her phone number? I want to call her. I want her to visit me." Blah, blah, blah, and on and on.

I knew that's what she'd say, and all those years, that's why I never told her. I didn't want to have to say, "I don't know where she is. I don't even know her name. I never tried to find her." I couldn't tell my mom that all these years I felt guilty that I never tried to find my own daughter.

You see, my mom's big on relationships — family letters, full of blah, blah, blah. Valentine cards. "Be my Valentine," for God's sake, and I'm 44 years old, birthday cards to everyone in the phone book whose name begins with R, Christmas letters up the kwazoo. She invented relationships.

I said, "Look, Mom, cool it. Let's not overwhelm her. I'll let you know."

"Oh, I'll wait 'til you give me permission." Fat chance. Like hell she would. She wouldn't give up 'til she had name, address, vital statistics and number of tattoos.

(HE hangs up the phone.)

Well, after that, I called Erin, my daughter, Erin, and she called me. We sent each other photos, and she's just as beautiful as her name. Blonde like her mom, but there's something about — the eyes and maybe the chin. . . . Well, the truth is, she looks like me.

One day she called and said she and Lori were going on a cruise out of Miami. Lori and her husband had just separated and Erin said it was a good idea if they just got away together, two gals on a cruise.

When we hung up, I sat there for a long time.

"Are you crazy?" I thought. "They don't want to see you. What in the hell would we have to say to each other except, 'You dirty rat, why weren't you there for me? You had your chance. You blew it! Now you want a relationship! Go away! Get lost! Get the hell out of my life!'"

A thousand thoughts went through my head. "You're a damned fool if you call her back and tell her your crazy idea." Finally I just figured, I've always been a damned fool. What do I have to lose now? I might as well play it out. So I call her back.

(HE picks up the phone and makes a call.)

"I was just thinking," I said. "I could fly down to Miami and we could have a weekend together when you get back from the cruise. Just the three of us. Just you and Lori and me. If it's all right with both of you, that is."

Erin didn't even miss a beat. "Sure," she said. "We already talked about it. We just thought we'd let the idea come from you."

(HE hangs up.)

So there it is. Who would believe it? I'm flying down to meet my daughter and Lori in Miami. Don't get me wrong. I'm not trying to grab hold of pieces of my past, not trying to put that puzzle together. I already let that go. I blew it. So I can't pretend I'm not scared. A thousand thoughts are going through my head.

All of my buddies have said, "You're crazy. Why open yourself to the disappointment. What are you trying to prove?"

Yeah, what am I trying to prove? That here I am. That I've stopped running. That this is a whole new ball game, and this time I don't want to strike out. I know in my guts, whatever happens, whatever they say — "you dirty rat!" — the whole nine yards — I have to go. I have to tell them — that I'm sorry. I'm sorry for all the wasted years we could have had together. It was my loss and — I'm sorry.

And suddenly, it was like a great weight lifted from my heart, a weight I didn't even know I was carrying. I felt like I just sprouted wings. I didn't need a plane. I could just fly to Miami. I could just lift those wings and fly, and I'd be almost there.

(HIS arms extended like wings, HE executes a flying movement and exits.)

THE END

APPENDIX

ABOUT THE AUTHORS

Jan Henson Dow has won more than 150 national playwriting competitions, awards, and honors, including an NBC New Voices Award. Her plays have received numerous productions, workshops, and staged readings around the country, and her full-length plays have been published by Samuel French and Popular Play Service.

As a Professor at Western Connecticut State University, Dow directed the Playwriting Workshops and co-produced Western's Festival of New Plays. She has been the recipient of a number of playwriting grants, as well as grants for the new play festivals. She also taught playwriting workshops at the Osher Life Long Learning Institute at the University of South Carolina and at workshops around the country.

Her articles and poems have appeared in such publications as *The New York Times, The Dramatists Guild Quarterly, Kansas Quarterly,* and *Indiana Review.* She co-authored *Writing the Award Winning Play* with Shannon Michal Dow, and they have just completed their first novel, *The Darkest Lies.* Jan is a member of the Dramatists Guild.

Shannon Michal Dow is a national award-winning playwright whose works have been produced and received readings around the country. She has been literary manager of The Playwrights Collective of the Country Players of Brookfield, Connecticut, as well as a play analyst and acquisitions editor for a play publishing company. She gives playwriting workshops for adults and teenagers. Her full-length plays have been published by Samuel French and Popular Play Service.

She has been a feature writer and editor and a film and theatre reviewer for various Connecticut newspapers and has served as a judge for several playwriting competitions. Her articles have appeared in

Connecticut magazine and other periodicals. She also has worked professionally as a theatre director as well as a graphic and scenic artist and designer for the theatre. She is a member of the Dramatist Guild (The School House Theatre Playwrights Workshop, Croton Falls, New York).

Robert Schroeder has won a number of playwriting competitions, including an NBC New Voices Award. His plays have been staged nationally. He served on the staff of *The Dramatist Guild Quarterly* and the Dodd-Mead *Best Plays* reference annuals. His reviews and theatre commentaries also appeared in *The Nation, Commonweal, New York,* and other periodicals. His anthology, *The New Underground Theatre,* was published by Bantam Books, and he was among the contributors to *Playwrights, Lyricists, and Composers on Theatre,* a Dodd-Mead hardcover. He has been retained professionally as a play/musical "doctor" for a number of Off Broadway productions.

James Pegolotti spent forty years in the academic world, moving from teaching chemistry to being an academic dean to, ultimately, a librarian. An avocational writer, his 2003 book, *Deems Taylor: A Biography,* won an ASCAP award for musical biography.

PRODUCTIONS, READINGS, AND AWARDS AND HONORS

Dancin' at the Apple Jack

Productions

2014, Sun City Community Theatre, Bluffton, South Carolina.

2012, Ido, New York, New York.

2011, Sun City Community Theatre, Bluffton, South Carolina.

2011, Farmington Library, Connecticut, Edith Kufta Productions.

2010, Derby Branch Library, Connecticut, Edity Kufta Productions.

2009, Edit Kufta Productions, Connecticut.

2007, Samuel French Off-Off Broadway Short Play Festival, New York, New York.

2006, Guilford Arts Festival, Connecticut.

2006, Hole in the Wall Theatre, New Britain, Connecticut.

2006, Conton Congregational Church, Connecticut.

2005, Short and Neat Festival, New England Academy of Theatre, presented as part of the International Festival of Arts and Ideas, New Haven, Connecticut.

2005, "Just Folks": Three Unique Characters, Women's Club, Old Saybrook, Connecticut.

Readings

2009, Readers Theatre, Show Off! Festival, Camino Real Playhouse, California.

Awards and Honors

2009, Chosen First Alternate, "Hell with the Lid Off" Contest, Pennsylvania.

2009, Chosen for Readers Theatre, Show Off! Festival, Camino Real Playhouse, California.

2007, Chosen for the Samuel French Off-Off Broadway Short Play Festival, New York, New York.

2005, Chosen for the Short and Neat Festival, New England Academy of Theatre, as part of the International Festival of Arts and Ideas, New Haven, Connecticut.

The Fourth Wall

Production
2016, Sun City Community Theatre, Bluffton, South Carolina.

I Want to Show You Something

Production
2014, Labute New Theater Festival, St. Louis Actors' Studio, St. Louis, Missouri.

Workshop
2011, Sun City Community Theatre, Bluffton, South Carolina.

Staged Reading
2012, First Stage, Los Angeles, California.

Awards and Honors
2015, Honorable Mention, Old Opera House, West Virginia.

2014, Finalist, Labute New Thearer Festival, St. Louis Actors' Studio, St. Louis, Missouri.

2013, Semi-finalist, Drury Universityh Playwriting Competition.

2012, Second Place Winner, First Stage National Contest, Los Angeles, California

Mike's Angst

Awards and Honors
2008, Honorable Mention, First Stage, Los Angeles, California.

2001, Finalist, Second Annual International One-Act Play Festival, Malibu, California.

Patrol

<u>Productions</u>
2010, Ruffin Theater, Covington, Tennessee.
2000, Henrico Theatre Company, Richmond, Virgina.

<u>Staged Readings</u>
2000, San Juan College Reader's Theatre, New Mexico
2000, Love Creek Productions Short Play Festival, Theatre Row, New York, New York.
1993, Playwrights Center of San Francisco, California.

<u>Awards and Honors</u>
2008, Semi-finalist, Next Generation Playwriting Contest, Reverie Productions, New York, New York.
2002, Finalist, Malibu International One Act Play Festival, California.
2001, Finalist, Auricle Award, Plays on Tape.
2000, First place Winner, Henrico Theatre Company National Playwriting Competition, Richmond, Virgina.
2000, Finalist, George Kernodle New Play Competition, University of Arkansas.
1999, Chosen for the Love Creek Productions Short Play Festival, New York, New York.
1999, Chosen for the San Juan College New Play Contest, New Mexico.
1998, Semi-finalist, Little Theatre of Alexandria, Virginia.

Putty Sing Is Missing

<u>Production</u>
2014, Sun City Community Theatre, Bluffton, South Carolina.

The Spiral Stair

<u>Productions</u>
2013, Sun City Community Theatre, Bluffton, South Carolina, Directed by Jan Henson Dow.
2010, Fire Rose International Play Competition, Secret Rose Theatre, California.

2007, Pittsburgh New Works Festival, Heritage Players, at Open Stage Theatre, Pittsburgh, Pennsylvania.

2007, 6 Women Playwriting Festival, Manitou Arts Theatre, Colorado.

Awards and Honors

2009, Chosen for the Fire Rose International Play Competition, California.

2009, Finalist, EstroGenius Festival, Manhattan Theatre Source, New York.

2007, Chosen for the Pittsburgh New Works Festival, Pennsylvania.

2007, Chosen for the 6 Women Playwriting Festival, Manitou Arts Theatre, Colorado.

2007, Semi-finalist, Drury University's One-Act Play Competition.

2006, Semi-finalist, First Stage One-Act Contest, Hollywood, California.

Strindberg Tonight

Productions

2011, Sun City Community Theatre, Bluffton, South Carolina, Directed by Jan Henson Dow.

2002, Kansas State University.

1990, Festival of Women's History, Danbury, Connecticut.

1989, Henrico Theatre Company, Richmond, Virginia.

1989, Wings Theatre Company (Off Broadway), New York, New York.

Staged Readings

1985, Mark Twain Masquers, Hartford, Connecticut.

1985, Western's Festival of New Plays, Danbury, Connecticut.

Awards and Honors

1989, First Place Winner, Henrico Theatre Company National Playwriting Competition, Richmond, Virginia.

1988, One of two Winners, Kernodle National Playwriting Competition, University of Arkansas.

1985, Chosen for Mark Twain Masquers Playwriting Contest, Hartford, Connecticut.

Trying to Get to Eureka

<u>Production</u>
2011, Sun City Community Theatre, Bluffton, South Carolina.

Phosphene Publishing Company publishes books and DVDs relating to literature, history, the paranormal, film, spirituality, and the martial arts.

For other great titles, visit
phosphenepublishing.com

www.ingramcontent.com/pod-product-compliance
Lightning Source LLC
LaVergne TN
LVHW051500080426
835509LV00017B/1837